Contesting Constructed Indian-ness

Contesting Constructed Indian-ness

The Intersection of the Frontier, Masculinity, and Whiteness in Native American Mascot Representations

Michael Taylor

LEXINGTON BOOKS
Lanham • Boulder • New York • Toronto • Plymouth, UK

Published by Lexington Books
A wholly owned subsidiary of The Rowman & Littlefield Publishing Group, Inc.
4501 Forbes Boulevard, Suite 200, Lanham, Maryland 20706
www.rowman.com

10 Thornbury Road, Plymouth PL6 7PP, United Kingdom

British Library Cataloguing in Publication Information Available

Library of Congress Cataloging-in-Publication Data

Library of Congress Cataloging-in-Publication Data Is Available
ISBN 978-0-7391-7864-5 (cloth : alk. paper) -- ISBN 978-0-7391-7865-2 (electronic)

∞™ The paper used in this publication meets the minimum requirements of American
National Standard for Information Sciences Permanence of Paper for Printed Library
Materials, ANSI/NISO Z39.48-1992.

Contents

Contesting Constructed Indian-ness

The Intersection of the Frontier, Masculinity, and Whiteness in Native American Mascot Representations

I sat midway up in the bleachers of the school gymnasium, in the eighth grader's section of seats, for we had been seated by grade level by the teachers and staff of the Salamanca City School District Junior-Senior High School (SHS) we attended. We students had been gathered together for an event and were waiting in anticipation for the spectacle to begin. The gathering of students was part of a ritual that honored the Salamanca High School Warriors athletes. The event was a pep rally for the high school's football team and their upcoming contest with an archrival as a home game that was to be played under the lights on Saturday night, at Veteran's Memorial Park, the home field for the Salamanca High School (SHS) Warriors.

The cheerleaders gathered together and spouted their chants and rhymes in support of the team. These girls had congregated at the far end of the gym from where my section was sitting in the stands; those doors behind them went into the girl's locker room and were diagonally opposite to us sitting by the boy's room entrance in the gymnasium floor layout. That particular entrance was to my left and below me from where I had been sitting in the gym. Across from us, the rest of the high school grades sat along the south side bleachers. As the girls cheered and shook their pom-poms in readiness and anticipation of the event, the teachers encouraged the students in the bleachers to stand and honor the squad of players. Then, from behind the doors, the varsity football team entered to jog around the floor of the gym to the applause of the student audience.

In a small town such as this, sports, particularly football, serves as a common ground for students, parents, student-athletes, and community.

Football has such a national scope of it as an American founded sport that few other sports tend to rival its staging. It is the largest spectator sport as its weekly broadcasts of the professional level of play is a high ratings achiever for network television. In the small town atmosphere of this place, the game of football is very nearly hallowed by its meaning of tradition, and of the generational investment of the community, for Warrior teams both past and present (Rychcik and Edstrom 2001).

Wearing their home game red-colored football jerseys the team ran a lap around the gym staying at the perimeter of the floor before the gathered assembly of the rest of the junior-senior high populace, then slowed their procession to mount a stage that had been erected for the occasion by the maintenance staff, built next to where they had entered the gym. The team had gathered on this small stage and they were standing up, and now were applauding along with the cheerleaders and the audience. The cheerleaders had not left the girl's locker area entryway, as they typically had in the past, to line the floor of the gym on either side in front of the students in the bleachers as was usual after the team had entered onto the court. They were raising another cheer when someone came out from behind the doors dressed in a white buckskin leather outfit and a long feathered headdress.

To my disbelief of the visual presentation or in awe at the supposed impossibility of someone "dressing in feathers" (Bird 1998) and being put on display in front of these particular students, in this fashion, in this school, in this city, on this reservation of the Seneca Nation of Indians, such a display seemed improbable. The young man, probably a high school junior, ran a lap around the gymnasium floor, all the time waving to the crowd with one hand. The fringed leather cuff around his wrist shook with the strands of leather fringe when he waved. In the other hand he held a tomahawk with which he waved at the audience too as he passed by them. The smile he had on his face as he turned the corner to run past the section where I sat seemed a real one. He continued on his route, encouraged to do another lap as he neared the finish of his first by the cheerleaders and from the platform holding the football team. The student section nearest him where he started out on his circuit was where the senior class students sat. I noticed some Seneca guys stand up and they had their hands cupped around their mouths as they shouted something to the young man in cultural "drag." Other students of his same ethnicity began to shout things at him as he passed around again. I was silent. The scene had overloaded my brain in a sense because I could only watch as he rounded the floor.

Such representations of Indian-ness have become multitude in the world of sports and athletics in the United States. This example in particular is troubling in terms of its content. By having the Native American participate in this spectacle as performer, it represents a form of institutional racism where the real acts out as the imagined and thus a juxtaposition occurs where the fiction becomes the reality and is substituted for the authentic. Whether it had occurred as Levi Walker, Jr., Ottawa/Odawa Nation, role playing as Chief Noc-A-Homa for the Atlanta Braves baseball team in the 1980s or the descendants of Seminole leader Osceola who carry his name as their family surname acquiescing with the Florida State University and allowing the on-field mascot to be called Chief Osceola, astride a spotted Appaloosa horse brandishing a flaming war lance in the present. The public display of the faux subsuming the real plays to the ethnic notions of constructed Indian-ness of the popular cultural expectations of white male viewers and consumers of this staged pageantry.

Again as he jogged by my section he looked somewhat puzzled and the smile on his face was not as bright as before. Still he waved to the crowd and the majority of them cheered and applauded the image of the Indian warrior as he made his way around for a third time. This time his smile was barely there as he went by my section once again, perhaps as more confusion set in his mind. As he ended his third lap he ducked back into the locker doors and out of sight of the crowd in the gym. The whole spectacle lasted a bit longer than a minute in length for the young man to make the three trips around the basketball court, but it seemed longer to me for I felt confused as well. What did I just see? Was it really Ike St. Bernard[1] dressed in a white fringed-leather outfit and war bonnet headdress that had run around the gym waving a tomahawk? Did he just finish "playing Indian" (Deloria 1998:7)? A real Seneca youth, dressing up in "Hollywood" costume to perform as a "live" Indian, been presented as a spectacle? It did not seem real but it had just happened. "What made him do that?" I wondered. When I first saw the Seneca student-as-warrior mascot emerge from behind those gymnasium doors I was taken off guard by the suddenness of the feat and when I saw who the performer was, I thought to myself, "Wow, where did Ike get that outfit? He's not a dancer that I could remember."

I remember being impressed by the outfit he had been wearing, all white, hand-made traditionally brain-tanned hide that included a vest, fringed fore-arm bands, leggings to the thigh, faux breechclout panels for front and back, and moccasins. The headdress that he was wearing was also an expensive piece. All the feathers were real eagle feathers that were accented by split tasseled ends; except for the black on the feathers, the item was all white accented with white fur, white leather, and silver studs. The tail of the war bonnet went midway down his back, and the fullness of the bustle piece for the main part of the headdress was filled by the feathers. Tassels also hung from the sides of the mirrored temples of the headdress and fell to his vest. I was considering the expense of work for such an outfit and who on the reservation would lend Ike the attire. All these items together represented one labor-intensive ensemble that he wore, and, along with the necessary tomahawk to tint the spectacle with a marker of lethality and martial action, put on display for the Warrior student body to see and embrace.

As an expectation of popular culture notions of Indian-ness, it is the suit that makes the man, so to speak, and as such, a display marks Indian-ness through visual symbols of the Indian Other. Fringed leather clothing as conventional attire is one of these expected notions of the idealized Indian. Feathered bonnets are also a marker of Indian-ness that the consumer has come to expect in the popular display of Indian ethnicity. Although full feathered headdresses are typically associated with Plains cultures all Indians are associated with the use of feathers as ornamental and symbolic "decorations." Also, this performance was done in silence by the Seneca youth. This harkens to "the stoic" representation of the Indian profile, one where the silent Noble Savage is the context for this performance. Its silence marks it as a form of the controlled, manipulated ideal Indian. This is counter to the screaming, overly emotional display of the hostile version of the Indian, the Ignoble Savage. Here silence equals nobility in this consumptive display of constructed Indian-ness.

As well, from my personal experiences, when Native Americans don such an outfit and accompanying regalia, it is most often done for social cultural expression as in pow-wow style dancing exhibitions, not as a matter of daily dress or accessory. Such displays of cultural expressions are most often done in social contexts, not as a part of ritual association. [2] The public performance of constructed Indian-ness is quite often at odds with the reality of Native American culture modes, especially when idealized Indians are entertainment for the public gaze.

What has most stuck in my mind over the years is my second look at his face, the one where his smile was being replaced by doubt and a growing realization that he should not have gone along with this stunt, possibly suggested by the cheerleaders. After school let out that day, other Native American students questioned the young man about what he did. As for me, I was put off in needing to attend these pep rallies for the football team in the future. Even when I played football in my freshman year, I tried to avoid attending these events. Almost always, these pep rallies took place on Friday afternoons in the fall and I took the opportunity to sneak out some side doorway or unwatched exit while in transit to these occasions in order to have an early start homeward for the weekend. The display took on a side-show character that cheapened the spectacle even more for me, as was the exhibition staged for the mainstream student audience.

ROLE PLAY AND CULTURAL APPROPRIATION OF
THE INDIAN AS MASCOT

The reasons why the Seneca youth performed Indian-ness are pervasive. Was he doing it for attention from the school body both red and white? Was he looking for a fleeting moment of celebrity, of having a chance to heighten his social status in the school community? Was he offered something in return for his role play of Indian-ness? These questions had been prefaced above by those asked by Bird, Deloria, Greene, and Huhndorf, as well as a host of other scholars, both Native and non-Native. Why is "playing Indian" an act of "dressing in feathers" in order to "go Native"? Is it a larger question of cultural displacement and dislocation? Are those who are role playing constructed Indian-ness a synthetic "wannabe"?

The notions of *playing Indian* and *going Native* are the precipitate actions of the use of Native American–based mascot portrayals. How people "play Indian" and "go Native" with the aid of mascots culminate the processes of creating and constructing such mascot displays based on appropriating the cultures and modes of Native American peoples (Deloria 1998, Greene 1988, Huhndorf 2001). By becoming an Indian through role play is what playing Indian allows; it is the donning of the accessories viewed as Indian in order to act like an Indian in the stands or on the sidelines of sports spectacles. Going Native is a further step or distance in this process, whereby going Native, a non-Native person becomes the (white) Indian, assuming not just an alter ego through role play and cultural appropriation, but also of becoming an Indian in the flesh by internalizing Indian-ness through antics, behaviors, and accessories. This goes beyond the game of "Cowboys and Indians" as the person assumes and claims to be a "natural-born" Indian and wants to be and live as one with Native Americans as a member of the tribe or nation. From my own personal experiences of growing up on a reservation, there seemed to be a yearly summer seasonal influx of whites of all ages coming to the Allegany Reservation looking for a Native American communal experience during the 1970s and 1980s. This group of people seemed to be lured by the fact of real Indians living outside of the confines of the American West, living in the northeastern woodlands far from the dry, tumble-weed inhabited environment of the Western frontier. From speaking with a multitude of them as a tour guide at the tribal museum, many seemed to be content with being close to a living Indian, accessing tribal culture through an hour-long visit via tour of the facility. Others seemed to prefer to meet Indians on a more informal and casual format, hanging around after work hours to engage in a more social setting.

As a "wannabee," non-Natives historically have had fraternal organizations and clubs which are based on the social and cultural modes of Native Americans, awarding Indian names, "ranks," positions, and merits to their members (Greene 1988, Deloria 1998). The most notorious example of this process is that of Frank Hamilton Cushing, who adopted Zuni life for his own, insinuating himself into tribal life, and then after leaving the Zuni behind, continued to dress, and decorate his apartments in the Zuni style while living in the modern world (Thomas 2000:74–75). He was preceded by Lewis Henry Morgan who became an Iroquois by dressing as such and naming his role play organization for the League of the Haudenosaunee (Thomas 2000:45). Mascots offer the opportunities for the non-Native audience members who view and consume these spectacles to become an ersatz Indian, either as part of a large group function like watching a sporting contest at a court, field, or arena site (mimesis), or functioning as a gate keeper of Indian-ness on a personalized level of involvement and participation (alterity) (see Taussig 1992).

Why mascots are studied by white people is done out of the fascination of the Other. By putting on the identity or skin of another, the action by the wearer has contexts of intimacy which makes it desired to a degree. By using this agency, white males are able to become a different Other, one that is a more primitive, more natural, a more authentic persona than the one which they currently occupy as contemporary, post-industrial, modern American males. White males have been seeking a form of acceptance from within their selves as to the legacy of conquest and colonialism ever since it had been set in motion. Through the realization that these people have not sustained an indigenous connection to the land, their artificial construction of a nation covers over that lack of longevity through a temporal context which is missing from the connection to the land. This form of cultural impersonation lends a self-realized context of authenticity by the role play, one which legitimizes the copying of and access to the constructed Indian persona through devices and accessories like clothing and names.

It is in the studies of mascot representations where the issues of the positions of the uses of power are grounded. White males often study the idea of Indian-ness as expressed through mascots as a way or means of evaluating the notions of the Other. In regarding the constructed ideas of such representations of Native Americans, by studying the causes and effects of mascots, the researcher in one sense also constructs the path of the creation of an identity which is now undertaken by Americans at a national level of the discourse. This process lends to a view of Whiteness Studies as another means to evaluate the importance of mascots in the creation of whiteness as a concept,[3] of how it plays into parameters of race and ethnicity in establishing whiteness as a standard of normalcy (Newitz and Wray 1997:3). This will help to explain the mascot's factor of masculinity because of its white origins in the Euro-colonial mind. In the means of creating an archetype of a heroic white male, the mascot construction reflects the traits of the heroic white frontiersman who settled the wild places on the new continent. This virile archetype had the physical attributes necessary in order to combat the wilderness and tame the frontier.[4] Those characteristics which were viewed as worthy were borrowed from the hero archetype and endowed upon the constructed Indian mascot as an ideal by having the ability to emulate, mimic, and assume such an idealized form.

In the role play of mascot performance and portrayal, the mascots, no matter how Indian they look in appearance and in form, are always constructed through whiteness. No matter the amount of "authenticity" invested in the portrayal of Indian-ness, all consumers know that it is a white male beneath the costumed exterior. While in costume, often times while performing a dance routine, the disbelief of the viewer can be suspended to believe in the authentic Indian performer and its portrayal. "Through the familiarity and accessibility of these images, non–American Indian children and adults learn to selectively take American Indian identity as their own, to believe that one of the few times an American Indian identity is of societal value is when it is adopted within the context of a metaphor for battle" (Staurowsky 2004:24, 25). But, at the end of the reverie and spectacle of the mascot on public display, the covert truth comes to the fore, the white male is uncovered, and the Indian-as-costume is put back into the closet until the next opportunity to play Indian.

This role play is a powerful form of copying the Indian Other. Its power comes from the ability to consume the idea of the Indian and become it through this form of symbolic cannibalism. By figuratively ingesting the body of the vanquished foe, the victor takes on the imagined qualities of the foe such as speed, strength, and connection to the land or wilderness.[5] It is through this act of consumption that the white Indian becomes one with Nature, the mythic past, colonial history, and a continuing legacy of American identity in evolution. Part Halloween, part Fourth of July, part Columbus Day, and part Thanksgiving, playing Indian through mascot portrayals celebrates Indian-ness as costume, reverie, nationalism, and identity for the consumers of these ethnocized notions of Native American peoples.

METHODS

The foundations of this research project are grounded in the idea of the Other. Many times in academic research, Native American people have been and are still the subject matter of such investigations, and I feel that just as often as they have been researched they have been silenced, are given no voice, even when they are intimately studied and reported upon. My research is an attempt to reverse the lens of study, to turn it back upon the larger viewership where the ones who had been doing the studying are now the object of the research in terms of the text's collected data. This reflexive device then is used to qualify the way non-Native people have used the idealized Native American corpus to construct ethnocized notions of the Indian as a mascot device (King and Springwood 2001, King and Spring-wood, eds. 2001), and are now being studied by the former object of such inquiries.

The research is grounded in various academic institution locations that had former and current associations with Indian mascots such as Syracuse University who had formerly been invested in the Saltine Warrior as a side-line mascot presentation of Indian-ness; the University of Illinois who had been the home of Chief Illiniwek as the symbolic literal figurehead of the Fighting Illini; and Salamanca High School, the Home of the Warriors, a New York State public school district located on the Allegany Indian Reser-vation of the Seneca Nation of Indians. As well, a document analysis of the matter as it had been contested at the Florida State University and its institu-tional association with the Florida Seminoles as a business partnership of varying degrees is presented, as well as an analysis of the University of North Dakota and its use of the nickname and logo depicting the Fighting Sioux as its mascot.

The choice of Syracuse University (SU) as a contested site came about through a graduate class project for one course that looked at the history of post-secondary institutions. I had heard of an urban myth around Iroquois territories of an incident where two men from the Onondaga Nation con-fronted the sideline Indian mascot of the Orange nee Orangemen. The two Native men, according to the story, began to question the white-fraternity-boy-as-Indian performer at an athletic event at Syracuse University. From that supposed encounter, the sideline mascot was retired as a result of the incident. My research into the school's history of the mascot became the groundwork for my doctoral dissertation.

I came to choose the University of Illinois (UI) as a natural selection in the mascot discourse. Much debate on the national level of debate became founded from this institution's use of a sideline mascot and the performance of a "dance" that was the centerpiece of the university's fetish of constructed Indian-ness. I spent several weeks' time over the spring and summer of 2002 at the site collecting data, interviewing people, touring the campus, and docu-menting the history of the mascot at this place. At one point I was even threatened with arrest because of my investigation of the community's obses-sion with the sideline mascot.

The Salamanca (SHS) case was chosen as it had become a contentious site over the use of a culturally sensitive logo associated with the stereotypic notions of Indian-ness as constructed by American popular culture. That fact, and also that the school district resides on a reservation sets this site apart in the mascot debate constellation. The polar contentions between cultural tra-dition and public display are intertwined in this place where the landlords in this equation are also the local minority, and the non-Seneca community acts as a border town in the intercultural relationships in this space.

The cases of the Florida State University (FSU) and its corporate relationship with the Florida Seminole Nation have been well documented over the course of their contentious lives, and the more recent public aspect of the University of North Dakota's (UND) positioning itself as the most resistant of the sites has begun to come to light in its documentation by scholars in regard to its stance on mascot retention and use. These two places are remarkable in that both have tried to co-opt the local tribal nation(s) into an agreement supporting the institutional use of racialized iconography to buttress their positions in the mascot discourse. One had been successful, the other had not.[6]

These two particular institutions of higher learning have had the most controversy surrounding their positions in attempting to retain the Indian mascot logo and nicknames. The use of these images and idealizations about Native American peoples had been vigorously defended, rhetorically justified, and economically entrenched within their respective region or sphere of influence in terms of their geography and location. The control of Indian-ness through the constructed Indian body becomes the centering contention of colonial power as expressed over the colonized peoples that mascots inherently suggest. However, such defense of iconography can take place anywhere there is an investment in tradition, a significant financial influence, and an institutionalized tradition of colonial expression of power and mythic revisions of history over Native Americans that will be demonstrated by cases in later chapters.

I had conducted personal interviews with a variety Native Americans whose stories represent local, regional, and national levels of perspective and experiences. The local perspective is lent by Sue John, a home-school coordinator whose in-school responsibilities include serving as a guidance counselor when necessary and as an advocate for the Native American students with whom she works. Her activist roots from her high school youth, one that was influenced the examples of the American Indian Movement, AIM, also served her as an alumnus of SHS who had dealt with her own episode of racialized public display. In her upper-classmen days, at a pep assembly similar to the one I witnessed Ike parade about, Sue and other Seneca girls were confronted by a white cheerleader who had gotten a hold of a Seneca woman's outfit. The young cheerleader had put on the dress and paraded around the same basketball court as the young Noble Savage had done several years later. As a result, Sue and other Seneca girls staged a walk-out protest of Seneca students in response to the display of cultural appropriation by the institution.

Another level of mascot criticism comes from Doug George-Kanentiio, Mohawk author and journalist, and activist. He and other Haudenosaunee college students had organized the protest of the Syracuse University mascot, the Saltine Warrior, a fringed leather-clothed, war bonnet wearing faux rendition of the Onondaga-as-Noble Savage. His and the action of the other Native American students led to the retirement of the Saltine Warrior and this example serves as one of the models of mascot retirement. The regional context is noted by the influence of Syracuse University in the northeastern United States. From its actions, SU also is referenced in the mascot debate and is recognized for its early retiring of its Indian mascot. In this timeframe, it was the height of Native American protests overall, George-Kanentiio had learned valuable lessons about gaining visibility for his concern as this publicity eventually helped to turn the university away from the dancing sideline mascot.

The national level of discourse is given by the actions of Charlene Teters whose actions at the University of Illinois helped bring the debate a much higher profile that in the past of the matter. Teters helped to raise the debate to a national review which also became an assessment of Native American–white relationships overall. Teters even had been profiled as "The Person of the Week" by ABC News in 1997 (Teters website). Through her effort of protesting the UI mascot Chief Illiniwek and taking on the institution as well as the Fighting Illini in all forms and forums, Teters brought a new light to the mascot discourse and by breaking new ground upon which to argue the use of racialized mascots of Native American people. Her impetus to fight the establishment via the academic institution was grounded in the esteem and well-being of her children who had witnessed the UI mascot performance and were embarrassed and humiliated by such a clownish spectacle. Teters turned that anger and concern for her children in a cause which eventually led to the UI complying with the NCAA policy in 2007, nearly two full decades after she began to highlight the issue at this place.

Also document analysis was a major part of the constructing a critical and historical framework in which to spread the debate across in order to create tensions and make connections of issues in the discourse. Researching the histories of the mascots at each site through newspaper articles, journal essays, monographs and collected edited volumes, ethnographic texts and from other media such as film all inform the critical structures used in order to situate mascots across racial and ethnic lines, gender, and space/place contexts. The document analysis provides for a skeleton of sorts on which to pack the critique of the issue upon.

In constructing a critique of Native American–based mascots and their uses by mainstream popular culture, the theoretical frames of whiteness, masculinity, and place locate the research's data which seeks to tell of how the meanings embedded in mascots are predominantly white society's creations which reflect the ideas such as conquest, colonialism, dislocation, dispossession, identity, tradition, nationalism, and rhetoric back to its creator's eyes. In taking this critical perspective I am turning the lens back upon the viewer and making it the object of study, to see how white males have created the mascots which are embedded with such meanings for this group of consumers of Indian-ness. In this reflexive aspect of study, the viewer becomes the viewed. The observer and the power embedded in this position as observer, is now being critiqued and rationalized as to why American white males are invested in mascot creations, both historically and contemporarily, and why Native Americans as the Other have been made a fetish and become a commodity through this process.

THEORETICAL FRAMEWORKS FOR MASCOT INTERSECTIONS OF MASCULINITY, WHITENESS, AND THE FRONTIER

In this document, I employ Native American studies theories to tease out the Native voice intertwined in the mascot debate. From this perspective of ethnic studies, Native American studies ground the ideas of cultural difference and of physical difference in order to structure a frame of comparison which whiteness can be evaluated for its investment in mascots and their public displays. As the primary lens in which to study the actions and behaviors of the mainstream public, the Natives watch and evaluate the non-Natives as to the constructions of the meanings embedded in racialized mascot displays.

Anthropology is used in order to structure the use of meanings associated with mascots and of the investments of such meanings as a device for situating the construction of the ideal Indian in relation to mainstream society. The sociocultural meanings that have become associated with Indian-ness by the dominant society define paradoxical views of Native American people on the whole, and they can be unpacked in a decolonizing context of mascot critique.

Other social science frames help bolster the critical frames of the manuscript. For example, economics plays a critical part in the analytical frames by contextualizing the values associated with the making of a commodity of the idea of the Indian as a source of profit and cultural currency in the use of stereotypical Indian mascots. Political anthropology is used to explain the processes of power as grounded through cultural and social policies that attempt to address the issue in social terms of difference. History is a connective element that allows for the sliding across time to connect theoretical frames to make cross-connections through time.

In viewing the data from this research material, I feel that there are prominent aspects of the critique of Native American–based mascots which illuminate this in terms of theoretical frameworks. I will use *Place* as represented by the Frontier as a critical frame because the conquering of the Native inhabitant went hand-in-hand with the claiming of the land. *Masculinity* will be used as a context of gender on the discussion of mascots as most mascot portrayals are predominantly male in their presentation. The meaning of race/ethnicity will be addressed by the concept of *Whiteness* and its shaping of the discourse on mascots in terms of the creation of the differentiated Other.

This research maintains the intent of examining the role of sports team mascots which are based upon Native American people and their cultural modes and expressions. Several themes are used to triangulate the parameters of the research data. By using the ideas of the Frontier as representing place and location, Whiteness representing race and ethnicity, and Masculinity representing gender, the bounds of the study will highlight the means of constructing sports team mascots in terms of the idealized Indian as it is conceptualized and created by white male society from historic and mythic experiential contexts.

This high school role play event from my adolescence provides an example of the critical parameters of the manuscript research and critique in total. The public display of "Indian-ness" as performed through a racialized mascot presentation brings together the ideas of this research document. The mascot performance serves to ground the ideas of Place, Ethnicity, and Gender through the power of the ability to "play Indian." The performance of this constructed Indian-ness occurred before an audience of Native American and non-Native American high school students; the display of Indian-ness occurred within a public high school located on the lands of a reservation community; the role-player of the display was a Native American student that dressed in Indian-derived attire to portray the Noble Savage.

In a reversal of the critical lens, I am researching why white American males have been fascinated and loathed by the idea of the Native American represented by the Indian-as-mascot. What is it about the construction of the idea of the Indian as the vessel in which stereotypes and sociocultural conventions are placed when regarding indigenous North Americans on their historic home lands as met by colonialist endeavors and the forms of nation-building? How have white American males of all ages contextualized their experiences with this form of Indian-ness as it is held by American popular culture? How is identity of both white men and of how Native American men are thought of by white American males, grounded through the construction of the Indian-as-mascot? In honing the focus of the research within a given set of parameters, the text will capture or corral forms of constructed whiteness as the idea of constructed Indian-ness is unpacked to explain the notions regarding Native American males from historic to contemporary manifestations of Indian mascots. As a form of white studies, this research traces the influences of the Frontier as an untamed, wild place upon the relationship between them and constructed Indian mascots; whiteness is as often set in contrast to this form of Indian-ness as it is compared with it as well; and, masculinity also is paradoxically influenced by the idealized Indian body as it seeks to control it through a legacy of colonialism.

Mascots are further perplexed by the commodification of the body of the Indian. Mascots have an investment in them of control through possession or ownership. Mascots can be created and constructed to fit tropes of colonialism, history, and myth-making in order to control the physical body of the Indian. This then gives the creators of mascot the ability to profit from the idea of the Indian to produce a cultural and commercial context to the conquering of the West and its peoples by "owning" the lands and the peoples living upon said lands. Patricia Nelson Limerick points this commodification process, particularly of people, resources, and spaces, by the staking of claims to the land whether as miners, land rushers, homesteaders, or speculators (1987). This process of claims-making through the staking of territory possession is a continuation of the processes of colonial discovery initiated by the act of Columbus planting a flag in the sand and claiming all the lands that he could see for the monarchy of Spain.

Mascots then are the result of conquest and control. In making them a more recent or modern phenomenon of mass-marketing and mass communication, they are produced to fill the space between whiteness and Redness, the space that was created by social and cultural differences. Mascots act and are situated as intermediaries as they move about among those created contested spaces between Native American and White societies, serving to connect the two groups in in those spaces that are controlled and contextualized by white society.

LOCATING THE FRONTIER

The first theoretical frame of location and space are grounded in the context of place or emplacement. From this framework, the temporal and historical influence of place through time has an impact as to why the descendants of the Euro-American settler colonists place meaning in the spaces which they occupy today. Mascots then reflect the social and cultural and economic investments made in the land over time in connecting the Euro-colonial settlers to the land, this group seeing themselves as the inheritors of these places which had formerly been in possession of the Native Americans. Through the dislocation and dispossession of the Native Americans from the land, a vacuum was created in which the Euro-American colonial legatees filled those created spaces and now see themselves as the "native" Americans, as the now-possessors of said lands. As the new residents upon the land, the settler colonial legacy makes a secondary, artificial claim to the land, one which is self-validating through colonialist ideas of control and possession and of identity.

Physical and temporal location is also utilized as a theoretical frame for the text. Place, thus, is another critical factor in the construction and meanings associated within mascots. The idea of space/place has historic and contemporary temporal significance and is embedded in the use of ethnocized mascots as well. Mascots are symbols of the reification of historic encounters between Native Americans and the colonial settlers coming into the traditional territories of the former. Mascots symbolize these historic encounters as a contemporary marker of those previous meetings between the two cultures. The locating of mascots is grounded through these contexts which makes land and possession of the lands a barometer of colonization. Historically, the frontier served as a demarcation of the reach of civilization into the wilderness. The concept of the frontier was the symbolic boundary between the civilized and the uncivilized and the Native Americans fell on the wrong side of this contextualized border line.

Place constructs build upon the notions of historic and modern nation-building. The former border communities which are now part of "civilized" society seek to maintain their historic connection through the use and construction of mascots by a process of "imperial nostalgia" via memory, emotion, and location (Rosaldo 1989). The frontier border became grounded the moment the European set foot in the Western Hemisphere and made claims of it in presumed totality of their reach of it. The lands remain, but the Native inhabitants are dispossessed and gone leaving a vacuum in which mascots in the contemporary then are created to fill the void and make the place less devoid through the idea of the "return of the Indian." Mascots thus serve to connect the past to the present, history to modernity, and the boundless frontier to the fixed contemporary nation. Mascots are then become the reified spirit of the land made into an anthropomorphic constructed reality that condenses the untamed wilderness and man into a controlled commodity that denotes colonialist successes through the body of the Indian. What were once settlements and border towns now have become cities and population centers and those places that are invested in mascot portrayals attempt to keep the past alive, in which mascots represent that past glory, and serve as common grounds for these communities to unite.

Within this framework of critique, time and space give rise to the notion of place. Edward S. Casey's essay, *How to get from Space to Place . . .* (1996), discusses the constructed abstract qualities of place to the concrete realities of place in order to ground the ideas of culture and experience as a reality of being in a physical moment. The person in such a moment of experiential reality embodies a cosmological space of omniscience and also has a quality of specific locality by being in that particular physical place, occupying space and time and thus making it a place, created from the fact of the actual body's existence in reality, in that moment. By combining elements of ideas by philosophers and anthropologists such as Husserl, Kant,

Bourdieu, Merleau-Ponty, and Basso to describe the factors of place in space and time, Casey argues that place is cocreated and coexistent with time and space as a thing which must be experienced and defined in order to have such boundaries in cultural terms. The Frontier then is a context of borders or legal secular limits, and of perimeters or natural physical limits. The Frontier as a boundary has historic and mythic elements in its construction which the cultural experiences of Native American and Euro-settler colonials are set against it as contentions over space through time.

In making an arbitrary history of a connection to place and to the land, the colonizer version of this text tries to make a deep connection to the land through the use of time as a longitudinal frame, as a function or process of coevalness (Fabian 2002). In reviewing other scholarship which helps to contextualize this idea, Keith H. Basso's work with the Western Apache people, *Wisdom Sits in Places* (1996), links cultural history, place, geography, and linguistics together to tell of a people's connection to their homes, lands, and places through their sense and understanding of geography, directionality, or their own particular cultural *Cartesian methods*, and language of place, which taken together as an holistic frame knits the people to the land through their historic time upon these places. For example, Basso tells of a community's effort to help a woman's personal and familial circumstances by telling her stories which conjured mental illustrative images "with place-names. That way she started feeling better. Those place-names are strong!" (1996:92, 93). In the settler colonist frame of reference, such place-names can give a sense of belonging to the inhabiting of the usurped lands of the Native Americans. This desired wisdom or knowledge is similar to a contemporary context, such as in New York State where I reside, of erecting blue-and-gold painted sign posts and placards which tell the viewer that this was a place "where history happened." In this context history as represented by the symbolic Frontier is a Post-Contact colonial construct, one which seeks to legitimize settler colonial existence upon the land and in select places.

By making themselves the "native" of a particular place, "Americans" now on the land, the settler colonists are building upon places which had been previously occupied and managed by the indigenous groups prior to their dispossession and dislocation from these places. How mascots connect and are used in this regard are that they act as temporal touchstones connecting the historic past to the modern present through the idea of the mythic Frontier. As the colonizing element of territorial expansion is engaged, one tenet of this process is the bringing of European notions of civilization to the wilderness by taming the wild places and peoples that are there. The idea of the Frontier as a critical aspect of the research serves as a boundary in this equation. It is a demarcation which shows the advancement of European civilization upon the land in comparison to the Native American peoples already there. The frontier as place then, locates the interaction of historic encounters between the two groups, colonized and colonizers, functioning under a "porosity of boundaries" which allows for these kinds of border-crossings (Casey 1996:42). Places which utilize Native American–based mascots use them as colonized reminders of the previous inhabitants of the land who are considered to be past tense and historic, and as reminders of the Frontier legacy of the successes of colonization and civilization.

In viewing themselves as the rightful heirs to the lands, the settler colonists use mascots to fill the vacuum created by conquest of the peoples upon the land, to remind themselves that they are legitimized in possessing the lands of the Native Americans, "for the whole of the American people" (Roediger 1999:80). Mascots become symbols of a history which ties the settler colonists to place in order to give them a sense of "home." By this, I am saying the those communities which utilize contemporary mascots do so as a connotation of the heroic legacy of the past, one which uses mascots as a symbol of progress of civilization, and of the ownership of the anthropomorphic context of place as the conquered foe of this progress. In legitimizing this context of history of location and the usurped place, the new histories of place as represented by mascots have nationalistic and nation-building subtexts in their use and meaning, creating a history that goes back to the origins of white people upon the lands, and disregarding the actual Native Americans upon the place, the Native Americans thus becoming a symbol of the past and of the cursory category they have in this new revised history of place.

A LINEAL PEDIGREE OF WHITENESS

The second theoretical framework views the presentations of Native American–based mascots which are contextualized by race and ethnicity. As colonialized forms of power, the results of the historic notions based on encounters with Native Americans through time are used to inflect the ideas of the Native American Other. Such constructs have been grounded in displays of social and economic power, physical or phenotypic difference, ideology, and politicized comparisons between one group and another. "'White' attitudes toward . . . land was . . . an issue closely connected to the possibilities of economic independence in the United States. . . . Not surprisingly, anti-Indian thought played a huge role in the development of 'American Racial Anglo-Saxonism,' the particular brand of 'whiteness' that . . . was intellectually ascendant in the US by 1850" (Roediger 2008:22). Moving from this idea of white supremacy, I will use multiple conceptions of Whiteness as another parameter of the critique.

Whiteness addresses the context of the construction of physical difference, those which are readily observable based on phenotypic variations between people. From the perspective of the Euro-American settler colonist, skin color, facial features, and hair type as concrete physical markers were blended in with more abstract examples of difference such as ideological tropes like the capability of Native Americans to become civilized in European terms; to become civilized and behave accordingly; to be educated and learn and speak English; and to become religious and learn to be a Christian. The physical differences between Native Americans and white American males, once subsumed in these criteria, then, become modes in which to bury Redness to produce an Indian that is white in manner if not physical appearance and color.

"'Whiteness' emerged as a relevant category in U.S. life and culture largely as a result of slavery and segregation, Native American policy and immigration restrictions, conquest and colonialism . . . while cultural practices institutionalized racism in everyday life by uniting diverse European American subjects into an imagined community called into being through appeals to white supremacy . . . helped produce a unified white racial identity through the shared experience of spectatorship" (Lipsitz 1998:99). Whiteness as an ideological practice of the Euro-American settler colonist grounded in the formation of identity is presented as a paradoxical dilemma as it rejects notions of the Indian as it also accepts contrary notions of the Indian in making a Post-Contact construct of identity. Whiteness is then able to measure itself in relation to the Indian and validate its self-perceived superior position by casting Native Americans as debauched societies and peoples. Mascots become the means to control the degraded humanity that the idea of the Indian represents to white civilization.

Whiteness is inclusive of several elements which define itself in terms of idealized Indian-ness. Whiteness as an ideology constructs what it is to be white in racial and ethnic terms; it contains a context of the investment in whiteness as a social process which reifies forms of social and cultural power; it defines what "white" is terms of skin color and of the hue itself and the meanings attached to the idea of white. Also, whiteness is regarded as a hegemonic constant, one that has global appeal.

Constructing whiteness in relation to mascots is accomplished through tropes, or in following coevalness and place, through created places which contain experiential and mythic contexts of the idealized Indian, is derivative of these ideals as they have crossed both time and space. Whiteness sees itself as having the legitimacy to define "Indian-ness" all the while in contrast to the reality of Native Americans and their daily lives and circumstances. "Many works on whiteness call for recognition of the ways in which whiteness serves as a sort of invisible norm, the unraced center of a racialized world" (Newitz and Wray 1997:3). Much of the rhetoric about mascots is the context of honoring Indians for embodying those certain characteristics which the non-Native creators of mascots see as emulative and immutable.

Language and physical difference serve as barriers between the meeting of Red and White in co-equal terms and circumstances. As Whiteness defines itself in relation to Redness, Whiteness slides in and out of the contentious frame in easy and difficult places. Particularly, in response to the colonial history of Whiteness and the violence that was utilized against Native Americans in order to secure the nation and apply its ideals of democracy and equality.

Whiteness is realized in relation to the Native American-as-Indian construct as a process of Othering. This discourse is grounded in a form of power that seeks to reify its ethnocentric position by relegating the Indian construct to a text that is considered less than human in the ordering of whiteness in regard to Indian-ness. As a temporal consequence, the use of the idea of the ethnographic present is overlain the ideal of the constructed Indian in this relationship. Categorized as an historic past tense relic of American historical contexts, the ideal Indian occupies the past. Along with that, the real Native Americans are hidden behind such a constructed veil, necessarily outside of the flow of meaning between the past ideal Indian and the modern present of mascot portrayal. Whiteness makes itself as a sustaining construct in its relation to the idea of the Indian. By making itself into what Indian-ness represents as an opposite, whiteness always leaves itself in the superior position while Native Americans are located in the subordinate.

MAKING MASCULINE INDIANS

The third theoretical framework looks at the ways mascots are most often presented to the public gaze as a masculine male version of the idealized Indian. White males have created an identity about themselves in personal and nationalistic constructs of idealized Indian-ness that are also paradoxical in scope and meaning. Masculinity then, is another theoretical framework which defines the construction of mascots by American culture. Part of this construct is the male archetype hero which has become associated with the process of taming the Frontier, winning the West, and civilizing the wild expanses of the new developing American nation. "Thus too the land, as imagined, calls forth qualities of character, themselves carried a physiognomy-the body of the white male, lean, sinewy, hard, taut, the cowboy as white male ego ideal. These figures in this landscape are intrinsic to the appeal of the Western" (Dyer 1997:34). Masculinity locates maleness and a nationalistic context to mascots by having the white male hero archetype transform, to become a white Indian. This is accomplished by the "dressing in feathers" of accessories which are viewed as Indian and are considered as authentic in their use by whites wanting to become Indians (Bird 1998).

The Indian warrior is what the white Indian strives to become when dressing in feathers for public display. As the white Indian becomes the Indian warrior through the construction of mascot performance and portrayal and its consumption, the past and present of the historic interactions between Native American and Euro-American settler colonists becomes condensed and interchangeable as one persona assumes the identity of the other and becomes that one through dress, performance, and display. "White male heroism is thus constructed as both unmistakably yet not particularistically white" (Dyer 1997:163). Combining the attributes of the white frontier hero archetype with that of the Indian warrior ideal produces a context of whiteness that is viewed as a more primitive-acting white male, one that can survive beyond the bounds of civilization in the wilderness, and in some readings of this hybrid characterization, out-Indian the Indian in terms of savagery and barbarism in order to defeat the Indian at his own game.

Mascots then are the combining of the idea of the white Indian with that of the white hero archetype, of the combining of the past and the present of Euro-American legacy of history, and the authentication of the white settler colonist on the lands of the former possessor, the Native Americans. Mascots represent history and myth in an anthropomorphic context that can be manipulated for tropes of display and presentation. Typically, these caricatures of the Native American often are sideline entertainment whose actions and behaviors are believed to mimic what Indian-ness represents to the consuming audience in the bleachers at athletics competitions.

THE TEMPORAL CONNECTION OF INTERSECTION

Time is one other contextual element in the analysis which has an influence upon the entirety of the discourse. Time is an item which can be manipulated. It has a reflexive context to its use and meaning. Johannes Fabian's application of time in anthropological research, his use of the concept of coevalness, in his work, *Time and the Other* (2002), he writes that time is a comparable context, that the viewer puts time in relation to itself, and that often, the viewer is perceiving a different frame of time when looking at another culture or people, one that is outside of or different from that of the viewer's frame (2002:34). Fabian observes that time is "not a 'thing' with properties, it is not 'there' as it must be created, embedded in a culturally organized praxis, [it] is created here" (2002:34). Temporal contexts with coevalness, the sharing of Time, where time is used "as distancing devices" that can be categorized as archaic, savage, primitive, mythic, ritual, or tribal in its application to an "other" time, and that Anthropology acts as a provider of that temporal distance (2002:30). He states that "coevalness is Anthropology's problem with Time" (2002:37). However, Fabian sees that communication

between groups or peoples creates shared time which in turn creates coevalness in contexts of synchronous or simultaneous time which is the same
physical time, or in contemporary time that is the co-occurrence of time as
typological time (2002:31). The denial of coevalness, by creating distancing
devices produce a global result, and acts to place the referents of Anthropology in a Time other than the present [time] of the producer of anthropological
discourse (2002:31).

The data are used to determine the relative influence or perceived power
that Native American groups in the debate have had on the discourse at the
individual contentious sites. Input, or at least the opportunity to voice their
concerns on the issue, is important for these Native American peoples to be
heard. What effect these groups have on the debate is determined by the data
analysis. Also, the proximity of Native American communities to the discursive sites is evaluated. The consultant interviews form the basis for the meth-
od of constructing the multi-level response or "voice" in which to speak to
the spectrum of reasons engendered by the pro-mascot contingent for the
retention of mascots.

LISTENING TO THE NATIVE VOICE IN RESPONSE

As a subtext of this research, a significant contribution is to document the
Native American "voice" to critique the positions held by pro-mascot contentions. In regard to the Native American voice, it is one context that has
largely been unheard from in the debate about sports team mascots, even
when they serve as authors, critics, consultants, and activists. This research
thus aims to bring this voice to the forefront by intertwining and connecting
experiential perspectives from local, regional, and national levels of the discourse.[7] This will be done by highlighting the critiques of this perspective
against the arguments made by those who support the use and continuation of
Native American–based mascots for public display and consumption.

These frames of the research's discourse will be crossed by the development of the Native "voice" to answer the claims made for the continued use
of Native American–based mascots by mainstream white society. This ethnographic voice will be taken from local, regional, and national levels of the
discourse about mascots as the speakers of these Native voices have experience in the debate, often from first-hand knowledge of the machinations of
mascot construction and use. These voices will also be highlighted by other
Native and non-Native voices in the debate. The research will also address
forms of power, the construction of identity, the modes of mascot display,
and the meanings associated with the use of them for public consumption.

One of the intents of the research is to bring to the forefront a Native
American critical sensibility to the arguments about mascot practices. As

mentioned above, often times the Native American voice on the matter can be diminished, or even silenced as to being considered in the multiple frames of the debate. Because of the interaction of the academic canon involved, often times the issues raised by Native Americans does not become real or heard until echoed by a researcher, a certified, degree-owning expert in the field. Mascots have become so defended and regarded in this manner because it is a matter of ownership that is bounded by the mascot portrayals. By this, I mean that the white male audience seeks to become invested in mascots because they are symbolic of the success of colonial enterprise, and this context is one where the owner of the mascot, legitimizes a claim to the place and history of the land: it serves as a marker of control of the idea of the constructed Indian and longevity of historic time in order to make real the artificial claim to the colonized place as a usurper. [8]

The Native American voice on the legitimacy of mascots is dampened down by the overall din of the debate. It is particularly done so by the reactionary voice of the pro-mascot contingent. The Native voice is often located in localized or regionalized pockets of contention with few national level voices that are publicly heard although they have regard to their status as a nation-wide voice on the issue. An example of this suppression is in recent regard to the University of North Dakota (UND) case where the state's board of higher education directed the UND to drop the mascot logo, an Indian-head profile, but, in response to this, the state's legislature and the governor passed a bill that made the Fighting Sioux logo the permanent symbol of the UND. This is in clear violation of the NCAA policy (2005) on hostile and abusive learning environment which mascots represent in their public display, and the state and the UND are seemingly ready to live with the potential sanctions by the NCAA in order to keep their Indian head logo. The UND is looking to upgrade their athletics program overall and compete wholly at the NCAA's Division One level, but if they keep the banned logo as a direct visual link to idealized Indian-ness, they would potentially forfeit funding, league affiliation, and loss of scheduling games and athletic competition. In August, 2011, after meeting with the NCAA, the UND decided to comply with the policy and retire the mascot and logo and nickname after the 2011–2012 academic year (Iowa State University web site: 2011).

This contradictory stance is contextualized by the claims made by the UND which states that the institution had the largest number of Native American students enrolled at their university in the state as well as the largest array of programs for this particular population of students (UNDISA website 2012). The UND Native American students' campus organization, UNDISA, had publicly declared contentions over the university's use of the Sioux head logo in profile. The students made claims about the controversial mascot logo and wanted the UND to retire the representation of Lakota people. After many controversial steps and missteps by the UND administration, volleying back and forth between retirement and retention, depending on from which area the most pressure was being considered, the institution finally acquiesced to retire the mascot logo image and remain in the NCAA, while stipulating the claim to keep the Fighting Sioux nickname. While the institution has made the decision to rid itself of the controversial use of the mascot logo, auxiliary elements such as booster clubs and alumni groups still use the Sioux head profile logo for some of the organizational activities such as the Sioux Kids Club in which three- to fourteen-year-old members receive an Indian head logo tee shirt, can participate in on-field halftime activities, and have meet-and-greets with university student athletes at certain select events such as the Potato Bowl game and parade (UND website 2012). By doing so, these organizations are not directly under the university's purview and do not have to capitulate to NCAA guidelines. These actions by these external groups point to the flaw in the NCAA's policy. There is no sanction for these auxiliary components that can be monitored by the NCAA. These groups can act as free agents in these examples. In terms of the contentions generated by an academic institution of higher education, the UND case had supplanted the position once held by the University of Illinois as a "most resistant site" (Taylor dissertation 2005).

The predecessor of the UND's position and legacy was the University of Illinois. This site, too, had balked at all notions of retirement of its Indian head logo and school nickname. A previous political move was attempted on behalf of the University of Illinois nearly two decades previous when in 1989 an alumnus serving in the state legislature proposed a bill that would keep the Indian head logo of the UI in place as a legal statute action. The resolution passed the house but was not signed by the governor, though he, too, was a supporter of the UI logo (Spindel 2000:163, Teters interview 2003). After much wrangling and ploys by boosters and alumni groups to pressure the UI, the university did decide to retire the mascot logo, while keeping the school nickname, in order to come in compliance with the NCAA guidelines. In its 2007 statement about the retirement of the full-face Indian head logo, the UI never once mentioned the efforts of Native Americans seeking social and cultural justice by ending the human mascot performances, rather mentioning the interests of student athletes and competition as the reason why it ended its dancing Indian practice (UI News Release 2007). Even so, auxiliary groups did manage to use university space to celebrate several "Last Dance" events to bring out the costumed character of Chief Illiniwek to perform publicly, beyond the scope of the NCAA jurisdiction, in order to relive its recently lost tradition.

Mascot protest had been part of the agenda for Native American groups to contend almost from the start of the civil rights era protests as a part of the Red Power Movement whereby the National Congress of American Indians sought to critique Native American images on screen, in cartoons, and by sports teams since the 1960s. On higher education campuses across the country, Native American protest of sports team mascots began on the Dartmouth College campus as one of the first sites in 1968 when Native American students there began to protest the use of the name, "Indians," used by the college (Ralbovsky in Hirschfelder 1982). Eventually the college changed their team name to the Big Green, one of Dartmouth College's school colors.

Some cities and states have picked up on the mascot discourse and have changed the practice by retiring Indian mascots as representations of Native American peoples. Dallas and Los Angeles, the nation's second largest school district, have ended the use of mascot nicknames (Machamer 2001). Wisconsin and Minnesota have dropped the use of Indian nicknames (Helmberger 1999). Also media outlets in Oregon have discontinued the use of such names referring only to the geographic location of teams that use such names.

The Native American voice has also been a part of federal litigation in terms of mascot protest. Suzan Shown Harjo and other Native American activists and intellectuals had brought a lawsuit forth against the copyright protections of racialized logos and nicknames in 1999 (King 2010:149). Part of this litigation claimed that names such as Redskins, as used by the Washington, D.C., National Football League franchise, disparages Native Americans and should not be protected because it is a racist practice. As the director of the Morning Star Institute, she was the named lead plaintiff in the *Harjo v. Pro-Football Inc.* case and won an initial judgment in her favor (Johansen 2010:163).

With all the data and ethnographic material collected on the contention over the years, why has the Native voice been so little heard? Who gives this voice the direction when it is speaking? As mentioned above, the authority is often in the hands or ear of the researcher. The credentialed academic is given editorial license over the material and has direction over the documented discourse. The power of the researcher is one that is precarious in that the prose must be academic and objective. By being even-handed in the reporting of the evidence, the researcher must be wary of leaving themselves open to calls of "going Native" in their perspective of the research material. This leaves me an opening as to why has Native American voice been silenced in many contexts of the matter. For one, much of the research has been conducted by non-Native academics. In being cautious of the potential "going Native" accusation, some of the researchers may have subconsciously deferred on some aspect of the research they had collected. In a field where one's objectivity is attached to their research, some of these people may be wary of their reputations, especially if they have been collecting data from sources that may still be regarded in an ethnocentric perspective by their peers as non-authoritative or as reactionaries thinking with their emotions rather than with an objective eye when commenting on the matter.

TEXT OUTLINE

The following chapters of the manuscript examine the material in more detail. Chapter 1 is a discussion on the Frontier as place. As the aspect of location and space/place influences the topic, it is the historical, mythic, and contemporary environments which collectively have helped form a basis of an American national identity, one that is connected to the land as the ground upon which the white male walks. The contexts of the land as containing the basis of an identity is one which is grounded in the actual colonialism and dispossession of the land from the Native Americans. It is the physical reward or rendering of the colonizing process. The land represents the prize of winning, and then the creating a nation out of the wilderness and establishing order and civilization in its place. This discussion foregrounds the idea of the frontier as a place where the past and the present can co-exist in the creation and use of mascots, providing an environment to reside as an imagined location. The response of the multilayered Native voice contextualizes the matter of place and location of Native Americans in spatial relation to the discursive sites.

Chapter 2 will discuss masculinity. The majority of mascot presentations are male in context. As a symbolic white Indian, the person under the disguise serves to link white males to Indian males through accessory and demeanor. The idea of the white Indian as mascot reifies the ideals of the white male as the replacement of the Indian upon the landscape, replacing the Indian as the heir to the land. White male identity uses the idea of the Indian as an internal and external context to identity construction as the internalized imagined Indian has positive qualities to emulate while the external real Native American is a reminder of the results of colonialism and dispossession. One is preferred while the other is disruptive in this dichotomy of Indian-ness. Mascots then serve to link white maleness through the manipulated body of the Indian that acts as an avatar of the mores of colonial legacy. This is grounded through the use of the example of the University of North Dakota and its constructed Indian mascot representing the Fighting Sioux. This social investment in the Fighting Sioux logo exemplifies the ways in which masculinity becomes entangled in the construction of Indian-ness as a symbol of virile and competent maleness. The ways in which the UND administration, athletics boosters, and individuals had become defiant of change and social justice reflect the independent character and nature of the American male standing up for one's self as a desired element of the self-reliant American hero archetype. It is this archetype which informs masculine behaviors and attitudes drawn from the Native American-as-ideal-Indian example and personified through the masculine hero surviving in civilized society.

Chapter 3 discusses the concept of ethnicity as grounded in Whiteness upon the discourse. The ideology precipitated from the processes of colonialism and dispossession of Indian identity form Native Americans foregrounds white and whiteness as the result of it upon people primarily and on the land secondarily. Being white establishes the citizens of the new nation as a hegemony which is based on the physical, phenotypic differences of people, one which is used to establish power relationships based in colonizing preferences of skin color. The distinction of being white makes claims upon a nationalistic identity that prefers whiteness and the ability to whiten the phenotypic Other in regard to citizenship in a perceived white nation. In order to explain these actions, the ways in which white and whiteness is realized through mascots are connected through the contentions of the Florida State University and the Seminole mascot persona of Chief Osceola. Crossing these streams is the way in which the university and the Seminole Nation of Florida have entered into an agreement in which white racism is allowed and condoned by a Native people because of the corporatizing of Indian-ness as a public marker visibility that enhances the public profile of the Seminole people as it lends an Indian identity to the non-Native academic institution of FSU.

Chapter 4 will address the Native "voice." This section of the manuscript contains more ethnographic material taken from consultants who have been involved in the contentions over mascots throughout their personal lives and professional careers. The responses of the collective voice which have been condensed around three individual that represent the discourse at local, regional, and national levels. Theirs and supporting perspectives highlight the contentions surrounding the debate. Of note in this section are that some of the voices of Native American men support the use of mascots, particularly in a cultural identity aspect, one which sees the ideals of mascots that is something that can transcend historic notions of masculinity and become a part of modern native men's make-up. The Native voice responds to the questions and issues of race and ethnicity as they surround the processes of mascot construction. Mascots represent the ideological grounding of the ideal of the white male-as-Indian in its use and presentation.

A conclusion section will be a summary of the discourse. This section will review the matter, and suggest means to reflexively mediate concepts of whiteness, masculinity, and place in relation to mascot displays and their use. Mascots have been used to represent Native American peoples as true contexts of the many cultures and modes which they practice. Mascots have become a popular culture representation of Indian-ness which has come to color over the reality of Native Americans in caricatured cartoonish fashion. As one Native American tribal elder had commented on the mascot issue is that mainstream society's people won't take you seriously if you are represented as a cartoon in their minds.

Chapter One

The Frontier as Place/Space

When the Seneca youth dressed in feathers in order to fulfill the role of the Noble Savage-as-mascot, the place where he did so was on a reservation. This poignantly serves to tie the critical frame of place to the discussion about the white investment in Native American-based mascots. This particular Native American community has a handful of non-Native villages and towns situated about its lands. These five U.S. congressionally approved villages and towns are in one regard outposts or forts situated in Indian land, and are representative of footholds of American society in the midst of Native American peoples and places. The performance of Indian-ness by the Native American youth in that space tells of the territorial displacement of identity that happens in the construction of mascots where the ownership of such cultural constructions are intersected with the possession of space in those places where mascots become invested by white American males. Their investment of mascot ideals can turn Native Americans into the caricatures of stereotypes that have been produced about them as colonized indigenous peoples.

Place is a critical frame of this analysis. Place denotes existence and relevance of humans in a given space over time. Place is contextualized by culture and history, of location in regard to space and time, and of the investment of place by a given group or society as to its importance as an environment and setting. Place becomes a lived element for people, one that confers a quasi-ownership to the cultural meanings associated with inhabited space through time. Place can act as a creation or genesis point for cultures and societies which then serves as a central point of reference for existence in that particular space.

The Frontier located as place ties together the longevity of a group in a given space, connects the past to the present, denotes a boundary between the civilized and uncivilized, and reality with myth. In this research the Frontier is used as a symbol of the existence of whites upon the North American continent. The advancement of Western/European/Euro-American society had been measured by physical as well as psychic distances between settlers and the idealized Indians to whom they compare themselves. The ability to create distance is accomplished through ethnocentrism which is grounded in power. This power is the perceived ability to create and appropriate others' cultures, modes, and idealized corpus and manipulate the outcomes or desired conventions of those appropriated cultural items and things. The Frontier represents all the lands of the frontier and all the boundaries acted upon in the process of colonialism and enterprise on the frontier. The Frontier is the idealized, mythic context of this space. As an ideal it is manipulable in terms of its abstracted meanings for the observer. It is a higher more nuanced place of fantastic proportions. The frontier is then more about the reality of the space as it is a political boundary that divides Red and White and that the border here is porous as much as it is imagined. The frontier is the practical application of the ideal.

The Frontier is linked to the mascots by the meanings embedded in them by the idea of the West as boundless space of unlimited potential. As a place, the body of the idealized Indian becomes a palimpsest or a tabula rasa on which to inscribe the ideologies garnered about the idea of the Indian (Casey 1996:14). The body becomes the central site of discourse as the mascot becomes an animate object which holds the contentions of the debate. The body becomes a manipulated trope that holds the preferred readings about the Indian and its Indian-ness. The body of the Indian becomes the physical reality context as the mascot presentation.[1] Via the mascot, the body of the Indian persona becomes consumed by the public. It is the idea of the Indian which is put out for consumption, and made manifest in the mascot and the accessories of the Indian mascot, logo, and team name. Whether it be done in the name of the Redskins, Indians, Chiefs, Braves, Warriors, Red Men, Red Raiders, or Savages, the particulars of consumption and the consuming of the idealized Indian are realized under the processes of athletics program boosterism, or of the supporters of the team, whomever is its alter ego.

Place and the Frontier are connected through processes of identity construction. As an historic space, place becomes a marker for identity construction in nation-building in one form. Creating a national myth embedded in the corpus of the idea of the Indian as the Noble or Ignoble Savage cum mascot, transforms the victim of the colonial processes into a trophy of sorts which is sported out in public like a prize, a token, or fetish. Mascots serve as a reminder of the conquest of the Indian and the success of the colonial enterprise, of the success of the nation-building process. So, as such, the Indian as mascot can be manipulated with desired readings of the good and bad Indian, at the whim of the conqueror, who is putting on display popular culture notions of Indian-ness such as when mascots perform an "Indian dance" at the halftimes of, or on the sidelines of, athletics contests. The dispossession and dislocation of the Native American groups and societies in the process of nation-building is a bloody page of American history, one that has guilt over the violence of colonialism by settler colonists as a facet of it.

One form of this guilt complex is that of cultural appropriation by the American people of Native American material culture and intellectual and cultural property. When mascots are presented for public consumption, they are made to fit within the trope of "authentic" behaviors and accessory. Robert Berkhofer Jr. points to a list of items that a stereotypic mascot embodies in its overall appearance like a feathered headdress of varying form, face and body paint, fringed leather clothing, tomahawk or other weapon, beads, and moccasins (1978:28). These accessories, when used by mascots, adhere to the conventions and ethnic notions of Native Americans by the American mainstream's popular culture. This lends an air of authenticity to the presentation of the Indian for display, and white America uses this as an opportunity to play Indian.

Place exerts its influence upon a people or society the longer that it is occupied and the populace has adapted to its land and environment. A context of the transformation of space to place is the changes made in the land by human existence there. Place becomes a part of the people and vice versa.

The idea of the Frontier as an idealized place as thought of by the Euro-colonialists is likening it to a Utopia, or a "no place" as it is only imagined (Wallace 1986:8). The Frontier, however, was a place of cultural contact and dispersion among the indigenous populations and the colonial settlers, it was a very real place. The Frontier also had a liquid, fluid quality to it as it was mobile and was able to be moved from one place to the next as was necessary to do so for the settler colonials understanding of it. It, like a wash of a wave of water, could engulf space and land areas, surrounding and finally submerging them within a nationalistic rubric of possession and control.

The Frontier analogy can be used to understand sports venues such as the field upon which football is played. There, colonialist interface between Native Americans and Euro-colonials is part of the contextualization of the conquering of the land. Football, then, is a natural fit onto this ideal as it is about gaining and controlling ground, to accumulate territory to the ends of seeking and securing a goal, and of securing the advancement of sides in order to gain land. Sports teams which utilize mascots as symbols of their teams, or sides of the conflict, are invested in the paradoxical nature of Indian-ness as the Noble or Ignoble Savage representations of mascots. The mascots are used in the context of the substituted indigenous people who had inhabited the land. The mascots represent a controlled version of such peoples, one that can be modified and fit onto the preferred readings of Indian-ness as seen as necessary for whichever setting the Indian mascot is presented for the public gaze.

As a context representative of the Indian in American popular culture, the two versions of the mascot presentation, the Noble and Ignoble Savage, or the Good and Bad Indian, the two ideals also reside on both sides of the frontier boundary. The Noble Savage, to a degree, is allowed to exist on the civilized side of the border whereas the Ignoble Savage lives beyond this border, residing in the uncivilized territory, or the far side of the boundary. By this reasoning, the approved context of Indian-ness as represented by the Noble Savage is an acceptable form of the Indian. The Noble Savage is one which is allowed to exist in this space for it is the romanticized Indian. It is the one which is emulated by the meanings attached to it in regard to constructed mascot ideals of the Other. The Ignoble Savage is the vilified version of the ideal, one which is held at a distance and is used to cause fright and impress the athletic teams that oppose the Indians, Braves, Chiefs, Redskins, and others, who have adopted such personas of the Indian Other.

Mascots then live at the fringes or boundaries of American popular culture and Native Americans, too, reside at the outside edges of mainstream society. However, mascots are the preferred form of Indian-ness, one that is *pro forma* to Western male idealizations of it, and real Native Americans are on the outside of this social construct, viewed as unmanageable in those social terms. Here, then, mascots become symbolic, the preferred forms of Indian-ness as ascribed by white men whom are using the mascots as a reflective mirror which shows them that they are legitimate upon the land as heirs to the materiality of this place via constructed Indian-ness.

According to Frederick Jackson Turner's "Frontier Thesis," America had made a significant cultural and temporal break to distinguish a "before and after" comparison of a "Pre-" time that symbolized the frontier, and of a "Post-" time that represented modernity (Deloria 1998:105). Turner's declaration that the year 1890 represented the closing or the end of the frontier also coincided with the closing of the "Indian Wars" era on the frontier as well with the death of Oglala Lakota leader Sitting Bull and the massacre of Chief Big Foot's Minneconjou Lakota at Wounded Knee Creek on the Pine Ridge reservation in South Dakota. Derivatives of Turner's scholarship refer to the "unrolling carpet theory." This refers to the idea that democracy and civilization unfolded and rolled across the country's lands, and its aboriginal people simultaneously, covering both with a tide of progress that spread from east to west and that it was inevitable for Native Americans not to escape this onrushing carpet of civilization and modernity (Mihesuah 1996:11). A link to the "glory of the past frontier exploits" was searched for as the industrialization processes impacted society and the nation was seeking to expand its influence and economies outside of its borders. Here, national mythic history and cultural hegemony sought to create a new identity for an aggressive, imperialist entry onto the world stage by the US to begin the twentieth century. It became much easier to substitute a martial metaphor for a sports metaphor, linking gamesmanship to that of military success on the field (Rudolph 1990:381).

I would like to suggest that, in many respects, sporting contests like football games are reenactments of the "taming of the frontier," especially with those institutions which use ethnocized imagery of Native Americans and incorporate these ideals into their public presentations of their mascot performance. Just as the nationalistic story of the American West becomes a success story of good over bad, contested ground, or land, is won or lost in the game of football, according to a line of scrimmage or contestation with the goal of gaining enough ground to reach the desired goal or reward. As linked to the expansionist Euro-Americans taking and then controlling the land as they pushed westward to the Pacific Ocean, the land, once in possession of the Native peoples, became the currency to evaluate the success of capitalist America in gaining ground as a form of commodity. The line of scrimmage or contention, also represented by the frontier, was moving according to gains and losses on both sides. The use of said lands, over time, became developed and evolved from the stage of the frontier homesteader onward and upward to the level of agricultural development through to the urban and industrialized modern society in its evolution of land utilization. Football emerged as communal rituals of struggle and conquest that renewed loyalty and confirmed prestige (Horowitz 1987:119). In this context, the socially constructed world reflected through sports and athletics, tying a socially dominant perspective metaphor based on racial hierarchies and technological superiority to a culturally produced nationalistic mythic nostalgia of an open prairie and individualistic freedoms, is a reenactment of the idea of the winning of the West via Manifest Destiny through the political economy of racial signs (King and Springwood 2001:8). Within this framework, boundaries can be said to delineate the "frontier," the space between the civilized and the uncivilized world. The frontier represents the limits of civilization, of moral living, and Christian ethics.

The analogy that a sports venue such as a football field can be transformed into the colonialist interface between the Native Americans and the Euro-Americans, is a part of the contextualization of the conquering of the land. Football, then, is a natural fit onto this ideal as it is about gaining and controlling ground, to accumulate territory to the ends of seeking and securing a goal, and of securing the advancement of sides in order to gain land. Sports teams which utilize mascots as symbols of their teams, or sides of the conflict, are invested in the paradoxical nature of Indian-ness as the Noble or Ignoble Savage representations of mascots. The mascots are used in the context of the substituted indigenous people who had inhabited the land. The mascots represent a controlled version of such peoples, one that can be modified and fit into the preferred readings of Indian-ness, and it is seen as necessary for whichever setting the Indian mascot is presented for the public gaze.

The idea of the Frontier begins in myth. The Frontier is conceived of as both a myth of place and as a myth of time as well. Together, these two ideals place the frontier in a culturally distant location, one which must be reached or attained through the capture of it in both contexts. Scholars such as Richard Slotkin convey that "European myths about America were two antagonistic pre-Columbian conceptions of the West: the primitive belief in the West as the land of the sea, the sunset, death, darkness, passion, and dreams; and the counter belief in the West as the Blessed Isles, the land of life's renewal, of rebirth, of reason and a higher reality" (1973:27). This idealization of space/place as a paradoxical context, much like the Noble/Ignoble Savage concepts of Native American people, were superimposed upon them, grounds a schizoid context to location as defined by the frontier as a boundary. In some perspectives of the Western hemisphere, European descriptions of the new lands present them as a new Eden, which could be gained through the conquest of the inhabitants already there. This vision of paradise would be won by Euro-Americans through "savage combat" with those inhabitants by meeting them at their level of primitiveness or an even lower level of humanity.[2]

To achieve this primitive level of humanity, to get someone to become invested in this context of degraded humanity, one had to come to believe the "myth of the frontier." That is the conception of America as a wide-open land of unlimited opportunity for the strong, ambitious, self-reliant individual to thrust his way to the top" (Slotkin 1973:5). The onus of potential gain thus was placed upon the individual to make his way in this new world, to have this opportunity to become potentially rich and self-made on these new open lands and its resources and material wealth. "[T]he ultimate development of the terms of the…myth, in fact restore original elements of the dream of the West that impelled the first discoverers-the dream of the mystic islands in the ocean-sea that hold both the possibility of eternal bliss and godlike power and the potential for utter death and damnation" (Slotkin 1973:539). Shari Huhndorf observes that in this context of acquisition and control of the land, White America essentially "owned" Native America for "it appropriated Native America for its national past . . . this myth of America gone native at once made the nation unique and shielded it from criticisms of its violent history" (2001:5). Indeed, the contexts of violence become subsumed in the recounting of the American historic founding to the point that "the myth of regeneration through violence became the structuring metaphor of the American experience" (Slotkin 1973:5).

Slotkin's theme of a continual, regenerative violence in the context of colonialism is carried through the winning of the West. As nationalistic story of nation-building in American history, conquest and violence go hand-in-hand, that there is not any form of colonialism that is not imbued with conflict and contention. As Slotkin views this process each step of the colonial settler upon and across the land is taken in potential and realized violence, of conflict with indigenous people defending their interests as they are set in opposition to that of the settlers seeking to gain and control the lands of the frontier in order to make the Frontier safe for civilization. "Classic" images of this cultural conflict include flaming arrows, attacking of outposts such as trading posts and forts, hordes of wild Indians sweeping over the ridgelines and down upon settlers' wagon trains, the burning of the wagons circled about one another, and the stealing of white women and captives by the charging hordes of savages. Re-enacted through Wild West shows, founded before the end of and after the Indian Wars era, this put the taming of the West and the wild Indians on display in confined, controlled venues which promoted the success of the American nation.

The regeneration through violence discussed by Slotkin is evidenced in the type of behavior described by Charlene Teters in the following account:

> It is like when they go somewhere else, you know, that people do things to them, you know, because they are "the Indians." They have to scalp the Indians they have to burn the Indians at the stake. They have to, you know, do these cheer leading antics, you know, that where they degrade and dehumanize Indian people. (Teters interview 2003)

Through the conquering of the land and the subsequent colonizing of the indigenous people allows for the assuming of the idea of the conquered by the conqueror. This form of power is a physical symbol of the success of colonization. As a form of power it is based in violence and is covert in the presentation of mascot displays as the Indian presented in these forums is a white construction of Indian-ness. Here, the manipulating of the Indian body reflects the desires of the manipulating of the land in terms of controlling and owning Indian-ness through possession of the grounds on which they lived.

Charlene Teters comments on the ubiquitous nature of mascot portrayals across the country:

> You know, I hear that all the time, you know, it's like all over the country. I hear it is like my story is just repeated all over the country. And sometimes it is a lot worse, I mean, I have heard of things a lot worse in terms of what these families are having to tolerate in these communities and it just amazes me that it is so invisible that people they just don't see it. (Teters interview 2003)

From her experiences, Teters has encountered the resistance to change mascots from around the country. She knows of the contentions which arise from the discourse on a personal level. Teters has been criticized on a personal level such as having anonymous hate calls, death threats, and being spit upon at protests she organized against mascots. The space she entered into as a disruptive agent was a hostile environment to her as she made a case for the retirement of mascots such as the one in place at the University of Illinois while she had attended there as a graduate student in the fine arts program. This hostile space in which she entered was one which was defended by the pro-mascot contingent as a normative place for their views and conventions about Native Americans, defended by them as a place of white privilege and white supremacy. From this national level of discourse, Teters had been on the frontlines of the contentions of the mascot debate.

At one point, Teters tells of the hardships she was experiencing in a communication with one of her tribal members who was also a tribal representative at the time:

> I am starting to describe it and he is laughing through my entire story and I am going, "Well, this is not going too well," you know. And it is getting kind of heated and I am kind of worried that you know something might happen to me and my family. And he starts to get quiet and I am going, like, you know, and I start to talk about how threatening it is. That people are driving by and things have been left on the porch and in the yard and like decapitated rabbits and things like that. Things like that and he gets quiet and then he scolds me. He goes, "God damn, Char! Where the hell do you think you are? Do you know where you are? God damn it!" you know it, he goes like that. "What were you expecting?" you know, that kind of stuff. Then he starts laughing again kind of like, you know, he starts to laugh again he goes, "If they call and they ask who you are I am going to go 'Who?'" He goes, "No!" and I am laughing and he goes "Just send me a package of stuff I will share it with every council member. So we are saying the right things." But he gives me so much shit over that phone call. He says- first he is just laughing through my entire story, then he scolds me, then he starts joking around again about how he is going to mess with me and them if, you know, if they dare call. (Teters interview 2003)

In gathering support for her position, Teters sought advice from her home community. She received some levity from her friend over the tensions in which she is involved. He teases her by scolding her, asking her if she knows where she is physically, meaning she is no longer within her reservation community. That is, for her, working from a place of personal political power for herself. This was a subtle way to alert her to the fact that she was off the reservation, out in the world, as it were.

In the use of place as a critical framework, the idea of the Frontier has had many contexts of meaning and reference for the West. As Casey observes, "There is no knowing or sensing a place except by being in that place, and to be in a place is to perceive it" (1996:18). In order to claim the lands of the frontier, the original inhabitants had to be dealt with by the Euro-colonizers. To take control of the land away from the indigenous peoples, rationales had to be found in which to justify the colonial enterprises. David Roediger comments that the "Indian 'others' in the story of how personal whiteness came to be forces us to see the powerful and lasting ways in which white supremacy transformed settlers' identities by attaching itself to freedom and to ideas concerning gender. . . . The logic of dispossession bespoke changes in how 'whites' thought of themselves, their households, and of their lands, as well as how they thought of those removed from the land" (2008:12). In order to justify this dispossession of Native Americans from the lands, European settlers relied upon the idea that control of the land required a labor intensive agrarian mode to make a legitimate claim to the soil. From the perspective of European colonists, Native Americans did not husband or manage the available resources, therefore, they could be said to not be in possession of the lands.

In taming the new continent, the frontier became a symbol of progress. Civilization's extent followed the boundary line ideally, and all items on one side of the line were considered conquered and tamed, made safe for civilization and its mores. In this construct America was tamed by settlement. The wild places and people were becoming controlled and thus bountiful. In this view, "America was such a chaos. Her natural wealth was there for the taking because it was there for the ordering. So were her natural men" (Pearce 1988:3). In the nineteenth century expansion was girded by the removal of the indigenous peoples out of the way of progress to make room and way for westward expansion. This lateral movement was following the land and its contours. By placing the Native Americans further westward beyond the frontier boundary, they could be ever kept at arm's length. "The removal of Indians from the lands east of the Mississippi, and then hemming them in smaller and smaller territories beyond it, would ensure that the republic would long continue to be built on Indian graves . . . and white supremacy" (Roediger 2008:63). With the removal of the Native Americans, the land was now presumed to be empty. With no one to voice any opposition to this situation, the nation claimed the lands for itself. "The allegedly 'vacant lands' there became for agrarians the imagined key to providing land, and therefore independence, to a growing nation" (Roediger 2008:60). To evaluate the success of creating a new nation-state, America looked to the control of the land and the resources and people, on the land as a measurement of its endeavors. In creating a new space for the Euro-colonial legacy during the nineteenth century, economic, ideological, and social parameters contained the elements of success as a showcase.

The frontier still held the quality of being the extent of the reach of civilization, and beyond it, the unsafe unknown. The fluid character of the frontier is an important element in the making a nation and identity out of the West. The nation-building ideal moved from founding a country upon newly accessed lands to one of fulfilling a promise, of making a nation and building it into maturity, to realize its potential for growth and the development of resources found there. In the colonial context of establishing a country out of the wilderness, wondering what was hidden behind the next tree, trying to maintain a foothold in that space, the whereas when setting foot onto the wide open plains, the notions of colonizing settlement in this space were to take bold steps out onto the prairies and grasslands as these open spaces had little opportunities to hide any potential threat that could be lurking behind a forest full of trees. In this construct, the frontier as the West becomes associated with limitless bounty and unprecedented potential for the settlers' cause. "The image of the frontier . . . is both temporal and a spatial concept, not only in the sense of being the period and the place of establishing presence, but also in suggesting a dynamic that enables progress, the onward and upward march of the human spirit through time, that keeps pressing ahead into new territory. Moreover, it signals a border between established and unestablished order, a border that is not crossed but pushed endlessly back" (Dyer 1997:33).

As an example of the investment of place and the connection of mascots that represent occupation and control of space, the University of Illinois represents the hybrid space of the frontier and civilized places. The state of Illinois represents transitional place in that it straddles the edge of the Great Lakes at its western edge and meets the plains and prairies at their eastern edge. Its place on the frontier is an in-between place as it is eastern as it is western. The legacy of settlers here is that in one ironic humorous context it is the place where the wooden wagon wheel spokes broke and the wagon went no further. The broken-spoked wagon becomes a lawn ornament and a symbol of the settler expansion further into the West.[3] The settlers stake a claim to the West as the East is at their backs. University of Illinois anthropology professor Brenda J. Farnell speaks about this cultural legacy of the West and East as it is confronted in Illinois. The investment of white men in Illinois of their historic legacy of being in the West though they historically stopped just short of the "true" West in terms of location. At the UI the mascot had been defended as though it were a coveted resource that cannot be duplicated and had been defended vigorously by the descendants of the colonial settlers.

> I really hadn't had taken much notice to what extent these mascots are imbedded in mainstream culture here. In other words, it's not just big universities, but high schools and small colleges all over the state and country. So I didn't realize the extent to which it was deeply imbedded in the culture. And that shocked me, you know, the kind of resistance that people had to change and how conservative this community, not the university community per say, but Illinois as a state outside of the university was so conservative and so wedded to this emotion attached to the symbol really surprised me. (Farnell interview 2002)

Farnell's observations tell of the depth the idea of the Indian had become incorporated by the modern UI institution. The mascot was not only a part of the education institution of the UI, it was also a part of every level of social life in Illinois. The influence and the iconic status of the mascot had become a popular culture stalwart that also became a form of identity for these descendants of the colonial settlers. Located on the Frontier, the Indian that was met in this place was also idealized over time as well.

The settings or tropes of the presentation of mascots reflect the notions of identity construction by white Americans. As a dancing sideline entertainment spectacle or as a halftime performance of Indian-ness, the codes of the performance liken the mascot portrayal to a puppet-like caricature, one that dances to the conqueror's beat, performing to a prescribed routine of body movements. As an avatar of national identity, the mascot reifies the constructed national identity created by the American nation-state. The parameters of performance are bounded within the ideals of American independence, pride, and cultural appropriation. The mascot in this example reflects the Frontier in the following ways and meanings. The mascot performer is most often of the Noble Savage variety of idealized Indian. This particular version of the "good/bad" Indian is the preferred reading of Indian-ness in that the Noble Savage is regarded more as the help-mate of the settler colonial, in the context of Man Friday, Tonto, or Blue Back.[4]

As a smiling aide of colonialism, the "friendly" Indian context happily assists the colonial enterprise with the dislocation and dispossession of Native Americans from the land. Another example is that the mascot is the more socially accepted version, one which is within the arm's length of social distance demarcated by white America. As so, this mascot variety is one which is controlled in terms of the trope of public performance and display. This version of Indian-ness is the kind who has been colonized and is now covalent with Western ideologies. Yet another example is that the mascot acts and behaves according to the ideal notions of Indian-ness conventionalized over time by Native/non-Native contact and experience. The antics on the sidelines of athletics events are the performance space of the mascot representative of these ideals. The mascot acts as a barometer of the mood and tenor of the fans in the audience watching the event. The mascot also serves as a gatekeeper in a temporal context, linking the past glory of colonialism and conquest with the present day context of performance in a space where fictive kinship relations are established. The connection between the past and the present embodied in the mascot brings the past success of nation-building together with the symbol of the conquered people, now acting in conjunction with the popular culture notions of Indian-ness idealized by its conqueror: the European-descended, colonial settler of white America.

Doug George-Kanentiio is a Mohawk Nation journalist. He and other Haudenosaunee students at Syracuse University mobilized and organized themselves to protest the university's sideline mascot, the Saltine Warrior. Their protests helped to change the culture at Syracuse University and it became one of the institutions noted for the retirement of its Indian mascot.

> The first time I was actually conscious of a thing called Saltine Warrior [was] when I transferred to Syracuse in August of '77. And it was a character, it was belittling too. It wasn't, you know, the image had nothing to do with the Iroquois. It was the kind of a Great Plains kind of dress and with the war bonnet and French buckskin clothes and things of that nature. And the actions of this mascot were cartoonish and I thought obscured real appreciation for the Iroquois, and the great tradition in heritage of the Iroquois confederacy. And it was just offensive, it looked silly. It was perpetuating harmful stereotypes and no effort was made to try to temporize that by the school by offering them a better appreciation as to this area's original heritage. (George-Kanentiio interview 2002)

George-Kanentiio's comments tell of the influence or its lack of recognition of the local Native American community, the Onondaga Nation, in terms of its proximity to the institution. The factor of the university appropriating "Indian" culture for its own ends is highlighted in that the idealized notion of Native American ethnicity becomes glossed over by SU's adoption of Plains or Lakota styling for their mascot. The importance of the Haudenosaunee by way of the Onondaga Nation community was disregarded in favor of a more popular culture rendition of Indian-ness utilized by the university. It is brought out that in this instance Indian-ness has only one mode of presentation as fictionalized Indians trump real-life Native Americans as a preferred representation of it. The frontier conception of the Indian is a more powerful idea than reality for American mainstream culture. As a context representative of the Indian in American popular culture, the two versions of the mascot presentation, the Noble and Ignoble Savage, or the Good and Bad Indian, the two ideals also reside on both sides of the frontier boundary.

Place is also considered in part for the influence of Native people and their location to these contested places. The proximity of Native communities of people to these sites plays a role in the critique of mascot presentations in regard to their physical presence. The histories of some of the contentious sites of the discourse had been and to some degree still are involved in the processes of nation building and colonialism. The historic legacies of place upon the construction of mascots at these contested sites foreground the connections to the past that are invested in by white America. These places, like the mascot as temporal avatar, connect the past to the present as these places existed on the frontier in the past, and now symbolize this past via mascots of local construction and meaning, putting these places in a betwixt/between space during mascot presentations.

In the case of the Salamanca High School Warriors, the betwixt/between context of temporality is a constant. In this example, the New York State public school district is located within the confines of the Seneca Nation of Indians' (SNI) Allegany Reservation of western New York. The frontier context is contextualized by the fact that the non-Seneca City of Salamanca is a tenant upon the grounds of the SNI. The City of Salamanca can be understood as an outpost on the frontier, located within Indian Territory. Established by congressional fiat in 1892, the city was set up originally as a foothold in Seneca Nation Territory. The city is considered a part of New York State, therefore, within the bounds of the city limits it has municipal, county, state, and federal interests within the community. Outside of this jurisdictional area, the SNI maintains authority over its own territorial land base.

A major factor in the debate over the use of Native American-based mascots in this community is the fact that the majority of Seneca school-age children attend public school in the Salamanca City School District. By doing so, each and every school-aged child, regardless of ethnic or racial background, becomes a "Warrior" by default of the district's and the high school's nickname and logo. He or she need not be an athlete to gain this status and identification, the child only needs to be a student. It is in these confines that the stereotypic and the culturally correct use of the school district's nickname, logo, and mascot portrayal have come into contention.

The historic contexts of the frontier, of "cowboys and Indians" games, and of the reality of Native Americans' lives are met within the hallways of this high school. As mentioned above, any student attending the high school is endowed with Warrior-hood by virtue of being a member of the school district. Some of the students, such as those who are Seneca, are doubly-endowed, once by being a school district student, the other by being born into the tribal identity mechanism of matrilineal descent. In this context, the gaining of a faux Indian identity such as being a Warrior is often in contrast to the reality of being an everyday Seneca, living on the reservation.

Cultural border-crossings are a part of the everyday negotiations for students in this district (Foley 1995, Taylor 2011). The ascribed status of being a Warrior is part of every student at Salamanca High School, which is doubly complex for those whom are student-athletes. This is tripled form of identity for student-athletes who are Senecas as well. The Frontier, whether in context as a real or mythic place, is constantly being looped and intertwined in the Salamanca community, as student-athletes are given status in the community due to their investment of time in playing sports. This perspective of history is one wherein the past legacy of colonialism is acted upon by the colonized people upon whom the process has been thrust. The Seneca students at SHS are under tensions that subsume their cultural and personal identity so that a broader appropriation of constructed Indian-ness is then presumed for all students by virtue of their enrollment in the school district. Here, Indian-ness is commodity tied to the location of the school district residing on reservation space.

Another circumstance that Sue John bore witness to was the hegemonic context of sports in a small community where football is the center of the sports culture. The generational context of football as a tradition is displayed through the longevity of the influence of the sport on the Salamanca community. The mascot is a form of power that reifies location and history together to produce an Indian-ness that is consumed by the community.

> In the community we have a group of boys—like eleven or twelve—that have a football team and their team or one of their teams is called the "Redskins." I've seen their name in the paper, and I personally am offended. I find that offensive. Before I went and did anything drastic or radical or made a big stink about it, I thought about it. I spoke to some of the parents in the community and I got answers. Some are offended but don't feel strongly about it. I would say half of the people that I talked to, that's about twenty families, haven't given it any thought because it doesn't matter one way or the other. They're involved with the team, they're involved, they do fund raisers. They're involved with the action of the team, not with the name of the team. Some are sensitive about it. There are a few people like myself that find it offensive. So, it's kind of a mixed reaction. I haven't chosen as yet to write to the Salamanca Press or to the district or anything like that. I wouldn't want to get people angry or anything like that, stirred up about it. Although I may do it in the future, you never know. (Sue John interview 2000)

Sue John's concerns tell of her stance regarding racialized mascots, especially in her home community. Her activist experience sought to make known the context of the word, "Redskins" in regard to Native American history, particularly is use in colonial times as a marker for bounty collected upon the deaths of Native Americans. This practice was established in the northeast by Euro-colonial settlers, no doubt including the lives of Haudenosaunee as part of the bounty system. Her reaction to a team of middle-school aged youth football players self-selecting the team's name was understandable since many team members were Seneca youth, and the head coach a former tribal councilor (see Taylor 2011:245–65). Ms. John's concerns were for the larger community and their understanding of the issues surrounding the word "Redskins."

At Syracuse University in the 1970s, contentions arose over the institution's mascot, the Saltine Warrior. Though the university's team compete as the Orange (a school color), they had been known in the past as the Orangemen, and were also represented symbolically by the Saltine Warrior. The Saltine Warrior was caricatured on the idealized Noble Savage, influenced by the locality of the Onondaga Nation, located at the edge of the southern suburb of Nedrow, New York.[5] The Saltine Warrior over time transformed from an Onondaga or Iroquois depiction with scalp lock and Mohawk styled hair into a fully Lakota regalia-styled representation of frontier Indian-ness with feathered headdress and fringed leather clothing as part of the costume. This became the dominant image of the Saltine Warrior as it strode the sidelines of football games played "on the Hill." Myth also was a founding element of the Saltine Warrior persona.

The part that myth played in the founding of the Native American-based mascot at Syracuse University occurred in 1931 with the publication of a story in the campus's humor magazine, *The Orange Peel*, in October of that year. The humor magazine printed a story of a campus excavation project that had unearthed some artifacts pertaining to a Jesuit priest who had been living among the local Onondaga people in the seventeenth century. Among pot sherds and cotton fabric remnants was one that had a profile of an Onondaga man with words from the Onondaga language woven into the textile as a caption that identified an Onondaga man as the "Salt Warrior." This image, which was put on the magazine's cover for the issue, was the rendition of the fabric piece's image from the excavation. The title on the magazine cover that went with the image was "Chief Bill Orange." It was at this point in the history of the mascot at SU that several of these iconic references became conjoined. The Indian image was a connection to the Onondaga people as the original people of this place, the name "Bill" referred to the university tradition of their student supporters (prior to 1931), often characterized in SU lore as "Bill the student cheerleader." Bill became so invested in SU athletics that he changed his surname to "Orange" to show his level of support for the SU sports teams. So, in combination with each other, "Chief Bill Orange" became Native American in the fall semester of 1931 and the image on the cover of the humor magazine became the image associated with SU athletics, college traditions, and of the cultural appropriation of a fictive kinship with the local indigenous people, the Onondaga Nation.

The power of myth is shown through this example as the fictive creation of the Saltine Warrior came to life on the sidelines of Syracuse University. The story of the archaeological remains of the Jesuit priest who had been living among the Onondaga turned out to be a hoax, published in the humor magazine as a faux story concocted by SU professors and the student editor of the campus humor magazine publication. A student reporter uncovered the hoax and the truth behind the founding of the Saltine Warrior in 1976, forty-five years after the Saltine Warrior first came into print on *The Orange Peel* cover. The "fact" that the original story was taken at face-value by the university community for nearly fifty years tells of the power of belief in the fictions of the Indian as held by the greater Syracuse community in general of the Onondaga people. The student reporter's story helped SU in its decision to retire the mascot during the intercession between the fall and spring semesters of 1977 and 1978, respectively. This information was also used by the campus Native Americans students group, Onkwehonwehneha, in its protests against the Saltine Warrior mascot. In viewing the actions of the university once the argument against the mascot was laid out by the protesters and their supporters, the retirement of the mascot occurred during the intercession between semesters.

By this action, Syracuse University had become a model for institutions for the retirement of Native American–based mascots. Much of this was due to the fact that the university had an active Native American students group. Another was that the administration supported the retirement of mascots from within their ranks. The Native American students group was also able to bring in the Onondaga Council of Chiefs to the debate as advisors, mentors, and role models. Also, the student reporter's story of the hoax of the Saltine Warrior's genesis was revealed, serving as a mitigating factor in the mascot retirement. As well as the college campus as setting for protest and social action for citizenship rights as a backdrop for these events to take place at this time.

Doug George-Kanentiio recounts his experiences with the mascot issue at Syracuse University. One tactic used was to shift the debate to the Onondaga Nation where the Chief's Council could discuss the matter and inform the sides of their resolution to the issue. The reliance by SU Native American students upon their elders is one form of tradition that was enjoined for the benefit of all involved in the contention.

> And so what we did was we took this to I believe it was in October we took it to the Onondaga Nation Council. We were that was the situation we decided to avail ourselves of a traditional Iroquois procedures for conflict resolution and we took it to Onondaga and they agreed to help us out. You know and this is where the remarkable thing happened. Well what we did is we decided we were going to bring in the, invite the Lambda Chi Alpha fraternity which up to that point been our most adamant critics. And they come in to the Longhouse and show them something that they have never seen before. Put them in another position, you know, for us would be a source of strength and for them would be something that would be unique. It would be to our advantage actually because we were familiar with the procedures and the Onondaga in many cases the members of the Council were the parents of some of the students there. And it would give us an advantage and would also serve as an attraction for the fraternity because they would see something they never had access to before which is a functioning Native Government. And maybe would give them insight to how Native People think. (George-Kanentiio interview 2002)

George-Kanentiio's reliance upon traditional forms of conflict resolution as enacted by the Onondaga Chief's Council tells of his conviction to the legitimacy of Haudenosaunee people and their methods of self-governance. The fictive community SU had been invested in with regard to their college culture made the students in attendance there all Saltine Warriors, much the same way this process worked at Salamanca High School. The reality of Onondaga people on which the idealized persona of Indian-ness is derived from in the academic world of SU, provided an experience in real life that wholly debunked the fictionalized use of Warrior-hood, Indian-ness, and academic hierarchy when compared with the truth of the Onondaga Nation as shown by the chiefs' deliberations.

Syracuse University was among one of the first universities to give up its Indian mascot. In contrast, the UI held on to its constructed Indian until 2007. The UI mascot became more and more of the center of contention as it became representative of the hot button issue as the Indian mascot issue heated up nationally. The mascot contentions at the University of Illinois (UI) had also become a site of discourse as the mascot portrayal became more and more notorious in the debate over Native American-based mascots. In this place, myth also was a large component of the grounding of the mascot portrayal of Chief Illiniwek as the symbolic icon of the UI. At the UI, Chief Illiniwek also is the symbolic leader of the Fighting Illini, the historic confederacy of tribal nations located at the western edge of the Great Lakes and of the fur trade economy of the seventeenth century. According to UI college tradition, head football coach Robert Zuppke is the first person to have used and defined what the word "Illiniwek" means to UI athletics. He is credited with defining the word as meaning "The Real Men, The Complete Men," in the Illini language.[6] These qualities he said are transferable to the football team players as they represent the UI in sports competition as they are "Superior Men." As a singular entity of sorts, the athletics teams, particularly the football team, become known as the Fighting Illini, derivative of the Illini Confederacy. The fictive kinship construct mechanism includes not only the football team, but grows larger to include the student body of the institution, as well as the boosters and fans of the UI teams. All Fighting Illini are led by Chief Illiniwek, the symbolic head of the Fighting Illini body.

The institutional culture at the UI allowed for such constructions of things Indian by the campus community, as well as the larger communities of Urbana and Champaign where the UI is situated. The Frontier is part of this process in that places like the Urbana-Champaign communities were jump-off points for settler colonists to cross into the frontier, to leave civilization behind and head onto the Great Prairies which roll out to the south and west from these two points. Thus, Indian imagery has been a part of this region's white settler history since contact and has been adopted by these settlers as part of their identity construct since that time. This association is further crossed by the mythic tale of Starved Rock.

It was an out-cropping of sandstone on the banks of the Illinois River that serves as a central point for this tale. According to the local Indian legend, the last of the Illini were driven to this high place by their pursuers, other Native American peoples, for their role in some failed venture. With their backs against the stone out-cropping, the last of the Illini held out until the very end. Some of the remnants were starved to death at the top of the stone formation. Other took a more spectacular end, leaping from the top of the stone formation, into the Illinois River to their deaths. Other variations of the tale have some of these Illini warriors surviving the plunge into the river, to surface from beneath the water, and steal away in the canoes of their pursuers, whom were watching from the top of the rock formation, and make it to safety. The nobility of these Illini warriors' sacrifice of themselves, not to be taken as prisoners by their pursuers, the uniqueness of the rock formation on the river, the fantastic ends the Illini were driven to, and the possibility of their continued survival somewhere out upon the wild frontier, are all touchstones in the development of Indian-ness at the UI.

Brenda Farnell, an anthropologist at the University of Illinois, provides insight into why such romantic stories developed about Native Americans at this point in time and why Indian mascots became so popular. She opines:

> If you look at when these mascots started to emerge, it's the end of the 19th century and the beginning of the 20th century. When native communities were now being confined to reservations and actual wars between Indians and whites, you know, have ceased for the most part and so it seemed like as soon as the very real threat from wars with Indians have ceased that Indian imagery and this whole idea of Noble Savage began to be used on University campuses and for sports teams and so forth. And the idea of imperial nostalgia relates to the fact that what happens in these situation is the indigenous people are removed and in a case of Illinois it's a question of what I call what today we would call ethnic cleansing what you cleanse all the state of all its native people. And then once they are gone and you have their land and all of their resources and they are no longer any military threat then you sort of get nostalgic for the people who used to live here before. You know, and of course you could afford to, right, you got rid of them. So this romanticizing of the past and creation of sort of a rhetoric of longing almost for an authentic position on the landscape I think plays a very important part in the construction in whiteness that blends Indian and white identity in the states. (Farnell interview 2002)

The national mood toward Indian mascots shifted dramatically in 2005 when the National Collegiate Athletics Association (NCAA) implemented a policy to end the use of mascots which foment a "hostile learning environment." Mascots such as Chief Illiniwek were under scrutiny because of the discourse about them and the influence they have in college campus learning environments. The NCAA compiled a list of institutions that were to be monitored, and the UI was on the list, along with other colleges and universities that had Native American-based mascots. By March 2007, the culmination of protest and controversy against the mascot, and the reactions by the pro-mascot supporters was ended when the UI retired the mascot in order to comply with the NCAA's policy.

Another example is that of the University of North Dakota (UND). This institution's actions in response to its Fighting Sioux logo and name had risen to take the place once held by the UI as a stalwart of resistance to change mascot portrayals. The Fighting Sioux had become the most public in their resistance to retire their mascot alongside the positions taken by the University of Illinois. As a result, they, too, were placed on the NCAA watch list, to be monitored for their compliance or failure to do so.

The Frontier is part of as the story at UND as well because it is located in the midst of the Lakota peoples of the former Dakota Territory region. This situation is complicated by the fact that UND claims to have the largest enrollment of Native American students of any university in the nation. In addition, it has a Native American Studies Program as well as a Center on Indian Law (UND website 2012). In a space which until the mid-twentieth century had seen a continuing conflict between Red and White relations, it appears that with so many real Native Americans on campus, the UND became more and more entrenched in the ideal of the Fighting Sioux as the historic, mythic, reality of constructed Indian-ness, which of course can be controlled and manipulated, one that is fit into the expected behaviors of the docile, help-mate role of the Noble Savage. In one regard to this perspective, that so many Native Americans on campus and receiving an education at UND, the Fighting Sioux becomes the standard of acceptance of the external Indian Other. The college educated, "tainted-by-civilization," real Native Americans do not fit in this constructed reality of Indian-ness. These kinds of Native Americans are those which are held at arm's length, ones whom are outside the social and cultural circle of ease of acceptance by the white society's mainstream. These kinds of Indians reside on the far side of the boundary that is the frontier.

However, in regard to the NCAA policy, the UND decided to drop its mascot of the Fighting Sioux logo and nickname in August 2011. After meeting with representatives of the group, the North Dakota state government will give control of the mascot back to the university in order for the UND to officially retire the mascot at the end of the academic year 2011–2012. In its actions, the North Dakota state government tried to usurp the authority of the NCAA by taking control of the education interests of the state body of the education department to legislate the Fighting Sioux logo and nickname into legal existence as a state law making the mascot a permanent feature of the state education interests. The state government relinquished its position upon finding that the stance by the state would jeopardize chances of the UND in getting into an athletics conference as the NCAA policy would find sanctions against the UND in terms of support, funding,

tournament play, and loss of scheduled games. The North Dakota state interests realized the potential loss of revenues by UND if it was to retain the
mascot, so the state backed away from its position of maintaining the mascot
through legislative means.

What had bolstered the reactionary position of the state's interest was the
legacy of athletics boosterism upon the discourse. In this example, it was the
influence and money of alumnus Ralph Engelstad. Engelstad, a former goalie
for the UND hockey team, made a personal fortune as a casino entrepreneur
in Las Vegas. He had made enough money to offer and donate $100 million
to the UND for a new hockey arena. As the mascot controversy ensued,
Engelstad took measures to ensure that the Fighting Sioux logo would be
prominent in the new structure. The first and most heavy-handed of his
positions was that he would take back the money for the new arena, at this
point about one-third completed, and let the structure sit unfinished if the
UND retired the mascot. The second action was to prominently feature the
logo in as many places that it could be placed in view of the public. It was in
granite in the team facility. The logo was placed on the end of rows of seats
in the arena, etched in glass dividers throughout the building, on team member's locker doors, and at center ice of the facility. Over two thousand logos
had been placed throughout the building. What comes into contention in
terms of the UND as an education institution is that "the Ralph," the new
arena, is considered to be private property, and is not under scrutiny by the
NCAA so the logos can stay on display there, while the team is part of the
public institution which is funded by public tax dollars and the civil rights
criteria attached to its disbursal and use. Because of the stance taken by
Engelstad before his passing, and the localized public support for the mascot
around the Grand Forks community as well as the support of one of the two
local Sioux tribes, the UND and the state legislature balked at the deadline
agreed upon by the UND and the NCAA from a previous lawsuit to keep the
logo, and decided to weather any potential sanctions upon the UND by the
NCAA.

At a meeting on August 15, 2011, in Indianapolis, Indiana, between the
two sides and the North Dakota state representatives all parties agreed to give
back their usurped legislated authority over the mascot to UND, and the
UND agreed to use the mascot for one final academic year, and for one more
hockey season. Even with a late push by the second Sioux tribe of a coming
vote on the support of the mascot later in the year, the UND will retire the
Fighting Sioux logo and nickname at the end of the year. A final nail in the
coffin of sorts in the discourse was that a group of Native American students
at UND brought suit against the UND for making a "hostile and abusive
environment" by keeping the mascot and the debate centered on the UND
community, and the growing backlash against Native Americans on campus
that are in the anti-mascot camp. Here, the control of the Indian mascot body

becomes central to the debate as older boosters and alumni try to hold on to their college tradition and the nostalgia that links the past to the present for them via the alumni monies and support which they represent to the institution.

An article in the *Grand Forks* (ND) *Herald* reports on one occurrence when the president of the UND attended a game between the UND and their intrastate rival, North Dakota State University. The rivalry led to an animus that displayed the hostile environment that is a central issue to critiques of the institutional use of mascots, particularly as they may affect Native American students attending such an institution.

> One banner read, "Eat shit Sioux." Another showed the geometric [design of the] Sioux Indian head logo encircled in red ink with a [diagonal] line through the logo. [He] must have heard the chants of "Fuck the Sioux" and "Sioux suck" 500 times between them. With the game won, a new cheer was born in the North Dakota State University student section: "Fuck their women." (*Grand Forks Herald* 1997)

A final example is that of the Florida State University Seminoles. The Frontier is connected to this example by historic encounters between the US military and the renegade Seminole Nation. The Seminole Nation is a post-contact construct. Refugees from various Native Nations who survived conflicts against the army and fled into the backwoods singly or in small groups eventually allied together against the federal forces. As refugees, living in the swamps and glades, the former Choctaws, Miccosukee, Creeks, and Cherokees banded together to resist the armed forces against them, they became known as the Seminoles, which is the Anglicized version of the Spanish word "Cimarron," meaning "wild things."

However, in this example, the Florida State University has gained sanction from the Florida Seminole Nation to use their tribal name and representative version of Seminole leader Osceola as an icon of the university's mascot and logo along with the nickname "Seminoles." The university touts that the mascot portrayal in one in which the university and the tribe had met to design and conceptualize the mascot as a public display for events such as football games. The outfit is made by Seminole women with an eye toward traditional designs or patterns in the outfit. Also, the mascot performer rides an Appaloosa horse[7] onto the football field in order to deliver a flaming lance into the midfield of the stadium turf to impress fans and foes alike with this display of authentic Indian-ness. Also, layered within this construct is the historic legacy of the Seminole Nation on the psyche of the American frontier mind. The Seminoles waged a resistance to colonization by the American forces for most of the first half of the nineteenth century, battling from the natural fortress of the swamps. In doing so, the Seminoles point to the fact that they had never signed a treaty with the United States and, thus, had not surrendered any of their interests, rights, or territory in any such negotiations with the Americans.

As a resistant entity the Seminole's story dovetails nicely into the stereotypic stoic Noble Savage romanticizing of the Indian brave silently awaiting his fate at the hands of Western civilization, accepting his future in whatever means and terms it held for him. By not surrendering to a larger force, the idealized Indian keeps his freedom and independence, his authenticity, by not giving it up for a treaty agreement. The Seminoles of Florida and of the Florida State University are in a symbiotic relationship with one another. Both gain notoriety because of the historic events surrounding the Seminole people. Both enjoy a financial advantage as the university is able to sell T-shirts and such with "Seminoles" printed on them while the tribe enjoys visibility via a link to the athletics programs of the university and their successes. Because of this relationship with the local Native American population, Florida State University is one of the NCAA programs formerly under scrutiny of its mascot policy. The Florida Seminoles have given their acceptance of the mascot construct at FSU, one which is derivative of a major historical figure in Seminole history, Osceola. Though the accuracy of the on-field display is fit into the trope of the Noble Savage, the warrior-on-horseback ideal is the preferred meaning embedded into the mascot presentation.

In comparing one education institution setting with another, the case at Salamanca High School relates to the FSU circumstance in that the schools tout their relationship with the respective Seneca and Seminole communities to which each is connected. The relationship between the Senecas and the district is one of location and of a contract with NYSED. The Seminoles have given written permission to FSU to use the name Seminoles and the likeness of Chief Osceola, with both parties benefitting from licensing of merchandise.

As a community focal point, the SHS Warriors provide a context of common ground for Seneca and non-Seneca peoples to connect. Sue John remarks on the views of Native Americans in that they are on both sides of the argument about the use of Indian mascots, logos, and nicknames.

> Within the past year on the state level there was a movement about schools that had an Indian mascot and the controversy. Salamanca has a team called the "Warriors." It has always been. That kind of hit home and there was a gentleman, probably in his fifties now, he made a strong statement and he's also on the tribal council for the Seneca Nation. He surprised me a little. His perspective is the name the "Warriors"; he sees that as a point of pride. He is not offended by it and he actually took a defensive stand in his letter to the editor of the *Salamanca Press* It was a positive thing, the name "Warriors" promoted an image of strength, pride of Native American men and he didn't have a problem with the Salamanca district having that as their logo. I'm not

sure how many other Senecas he talked to, or if he felt that personally as a tribal member. I've seen different degrees of mascots used on a national, local, and high school level. My preference is that we don't use Indian people as mascots. My definition of a mascot is an untrue or false person, or a sub-human being like a bulldog or something like leprechauns. I've always felt that a mascot wasn't ever anything that was taken serious or a real human being and I don't think Indians should be viewed that way. The "Warriors" isn't like that Cleveland Indians mascot, that big Indian guy. Their logo, looking like a cartoon Indian is not quite at that degree. We could look at other names fitting for our sports logo. (Sue John interview 2000)

The duplicitous nature of this commentary shows the confusion added to the issue when Native Americans are at opposites on the matter. Some view this context as a public display of culture recognition and pride. Other people can view the same material and find it objectionable to their personal perspective of cultural tradition. This can further confuse the issue as when outsiders or non-Natives see that Native Americans can be divided on the matter, too. In this context, some non-Natives have seized the opportunity to point out that Native Americans support mascots and that justifies the retention of race by them.

Place has much influence on the cultural memory of a people. The place as natural environment takes into account the factors of geography, geology, location, space, and time. These elements of the establishment of place upon a people act as two-way streets or avenues as the people influence and manipulate the land for their existences in kind. How place is established has a physical context in that the body must be in the place to create a sense of place by location as in being in the space in actuality; by establishing a temporal sense of place by the passing of increments of time of relevant meaning upon the body; by the changes in the land made by the bodies of the people; and by cultural patterns created in response to the physical reality of space and of the land and its environments. The cultural memory is then affected by place in terms of longevity upon the bodies of the people, through environmental factors like climate and resources, and informed by claims to the land through time and by physical presence.

Place then has a wide array of influences and perspectives from which to locate a people in space. Historical elements can help establish a claim upon the land. The manipulation of the physical environment shows an attachment to the land. Cultural knowledge is couched in contexts of the land and of its space on the land. Place is an intertwining of the elements which produces a place over time in a given space. It also has a linear quality to it as it connects the past to the present in an unbroken progression of cultural experiences.

Place is connected to Native American-based mascots in this research by the use of the idea of the Frontier as a critical frame. The Frontier contextu-alizes multiple forms of identity, ideology, and economics in symbolic and real ways in establishing the idea as a means of making a boundary between Red and White cultures. In locating supportive critical undergirding to the analysis, time is one example. In the construction of Native American–based mascots, mascots are used as devices which can connect the past to the present in terms of the land. It is the conquering of the Indian which gives the settler colonists a claim to the land and its resources. Mascots then are doorways through which the colonial past and its violent elements can meet the present and its nostalgic memory of Indians and then subjugate the historic violence of colonialism through the mascot as doorway now to a reimagined past where the mascots are the grateful Other in the present moment of an established nation-state global system.

The Frontier serves as a grounding point for Native American–based mascots because the Frontier represents the land that was gained during the nation-building colonialist enterprise of America. The Frontier is a border which defines civilized as opposed to uncivilized lands and peoples. The boundary of the frontier is one that had been crossed continually since Contact between Red and White cultures. The anthropomorphic representation of that endeavor, the body of the Indian mascot persona, is a fetish of those actions and as such, is a token of the success of those processes of nation-building.

As a result, the athletics contests which are football games are coded re-enactments of the processes of nation-building, of the winning of the West, in that the line of scrimmage is the border line, the boundary between the acquisition of land (offense) and of the retention of the land base (defense). This represents the Frontier in a symbolic sense. The shifting fortunes of one side or the other is reflected in the fluid dynamic of the boundary of the symbolic frontier moving back and forth between the two sides in the contest. The Indian mascot is used as a sideline entertainment gauge as the contest unfolds. The mascot serves to link the past colonial glory and power with the modern glossing of the former historical violence of the process of colonialism now as a structured game between two sides. In this the mascot acts as a gatekeeper between the kinetic, dynamic sporting contest of football games and the sidelines the boundaries of the field of contestation which football games are symbolic metaphors of conquest and dislocation of Native American peoples, and the stadium or arena seats, where the audience sits and judges the value and worth of the contests as an entertainment form of popular culture.

The contests provide for the viewer of the spectacles a glimpse into the nation-building efforts of Americans by witnessing the hand-to-hand physical battles of the individual players against each other, and of the plays and schemes in which to trap an opponent in order to secure more land in the contest. A martial comparison is apt for the opponent is viewed as an enemy, alien, and potentially lethal. Being on the far side of the Frontier is being located in Indian Territory, a place that is "on the rez." These historic references of conflict between Native Americans and the settler colonialists are part of modern day language, particularly in a military context as they were on the battle lines on these frontier conflict situations. Also, the tactics of the teams mirror martial concepts in planning and putting the opponent at a disadvantage. It is in this context that the historic frontier is linked to modernity through sports and games, and mascots are a translocative, temporal device that brings the two different time frames and spaces together.

Charlene Teters's comments about the media's use of the terminology from the armed forces contextualizes the power of place and the Frontier that the historical use of such terminology has a place in the modern warfare arena. The hegemonic discourse of the enemy still calls back into time of the conflicts between Native Americans and colonial forces on the frontier and brings such contexts into the present.

> Well, I have been concentrating mostly on educational environmental environments mostly personally and the reason is it's everywhere. I mean when I think about it, you know, it is so permitted in our communities and so much part of their thinking. You know, just watching the Iraq war and hearing the Wild West references and "Injuns in front of us and Injuns behind us." Did you hear that? (Teters interview:2003)

Place and the Frontier are both located with the complex that mascots represent of the negotiations and mediations of culture, identity, history, ideologies, and land. Place is a space where a shared experience becomes an historic context and serves to link people to space through time. Place creates space for people having a common experience which connects them through a fictive kinship located in time to space. As a physical environment, place provides for the establishment of a people and their culture to connect to the land and become integrated into one another across time. Land then is the grounding factor in which the fictive kinships embodied in the mascots exists. It becomes a common shared element which connects mascot supporters across economic, social, and ethnic and racial divisions. Through the contextualizing of the land as the frontier, the idea of space and distance become comparatively linked, creating a place for Native Americans, Indians-as-mascots, and white American men, in that order, from outside to inside of these constructed distances.

As the critical frame of place represented by the frontier has a great influence on the discourse because of the physical nature of it, place makes itself known by the actual locations of Native and non-Native people. Since the nineteenth century the location of Native peoples had been on the reservation. Whites were everywhere else, including residing on reservations. With the idea of place being contested in this fashion, what gives whites the power to reside next to Native Americans in the seemingly only refuge left to

them? The physical context of this construction leads into the use of masculinity to hold the power of these constructed bodies as a frame that is strong
and durable enough to hold the reflexive convolutions created by the two
ideals as they evolve and change over time. Whiteness supports the frame of
masculinity by placing power in it that reflects the strength of the male body,
especially the idealized body that conquered the wild places and peoples of
the land. Masculinity as it is represented by the male body and how it has
been constructed by the use of Indian mascots as a foil is discussed in the
next chapter.

Chapter Two

Gender, Masculinity, and Male Identity

When the young Seneca male enacted the Noble Savage in his display of constructed Indian-ness, his gendered masculinity grounded the public performance of a "chief"-like persona, in this perceived structure of men's rank and authority which is what the audience expected in its ideal Indian-as-mascot. Maleness is the context in which the majority of mascots are encountered. Indian males are considered to be more aggressive, bellicose, lethal, and frightening to the colonizer's mind in regard to historic and past experiences and these characteristics are what become embedded in various degrees when encountering them. For instance, the tomahawk held by the Seneca student symbolized this violent context of the lethal Ignoble Savage, the dark side of the idealized Indian. In contradiction to the war-like persona expected by the role play, the student's performance of Indian-ness was mute.

During the entirety of the time to complete three circuits around the gym floor, he never said a word, war-whoop, or grunt: he was totally silent. This context of public display is reflective of the same such expected notions grounded in such a display of Indian maleness in that much of the time the persona is deemed unintelligible by his failure to communicate, either silently, or yelling loudly, or speaking in broken or pidgin-ed English fashion. The mascot is no great orator of his intellectual discernment. As a Noble Savage, though, he really does not need to speak to be heard as his visual presence is often enough to evoke responses form the viewing audience. The sideline Indian can be recognized visually from across a greater distance than heard over the same space. Brightly-colored feathers and head-dresses with either tails or bustles, or both, can tend to stand out on the sidelines, and quite as frequently as head-dresses are used as part of Indian mascot accessory, the mascot may be sporting a brown outfit as attire. In one sense, such as a photograph, his visual essence is enough to speak a thousand words. The silent Indian male trope has greatly relied on posturing and body language to convey his thoughts or feelings or intent. The strong, silent type is what befits the mascot in this context of his masculinized make-up.

The idealized constructed Indian body speaks volumes through stoic posings and behaviors. His body language has certain physical positionings that can be considered "classic" and essential to this form of Indian-speak. He most often stands erect and stiff with his arms outward and folded, his hands resting upon the elbows of his raised and squared arms extended to chest level. Another common pose is the hand over the brow to help make it a visor and help to sharpen its vision. Another pose is the raising of the Indian's one hand to show the palm, facing outward, as a sign of presumed welcome and saying, "How!" The position of extending both hands upward, above the headdress of the mascot in a mimic of an "It's good!" signal of a score in a football game, is another prime posture. Or the running laps around a gymnasium floor to show off the mascot-as-idealized Indian's physical ability such as speed and agility. The constructed Indian can be made to fit into these physical positions within the imagination of the white American man's past historic experiences with the Ig-/Noble Savage. These positions and expressions of body language are to confer an imagined and commodified dignity and nobility to the mascot's manipulated posturings, those that are part of a trope in which Indian-ness satisfies the demand of the Indian construct. In this trope, the silent Indian chief stoically confers his acceptance of the display through his gaze back upon the American male, fulfilling yet another stereotype, that one of the wise old elder whom can give traditional knowledge through his knowing glance at the heroic settler of the West.

Looking in the area of rhetoric and ideology surrounding the Native American-as-Indian object, European Americans saw only grotesque confabulations of themselves, amalgamations of the colonizing European and the indigenous Native, figures that doubled one another and in the doubling divided and fractured, shattering any hope of stabilizing differences and therefore self (Smith-Rosenberg 2010:249). In the doubling and splintering of these fractured representations which then serving as mirrors reflect an alterity of the image, reflecting back an image or idea Indian-ness while it becoming grounded in the shifting historic and mythic meta-narratives of the Other.[1] The mirrors are themselves textured as bevels in the looking glass's surface providing a fun-house like, distorted reality for the self's gaze, doubling and doubling again within the shaped contours of these mirrors. The masculine reflections serve as connections to whiteness through Indian-ness as images of itself becomes doubled: it compels the desire for a forbidden male-male connection fused with the desire for an equally forbidden connection between savage and civilized, red and white (Smith-Rosenberg

2010:279). European and Native American identities are inseparable, sharing the same lands on which their distinct identities are grounded. Paradoxically, she observes that European and Native Americans are one another's interconnected dangerous doubles (Smith-Rosenberg 2010:279).

Gender is central to this work by way of the social representation that mascots serve in constructing an identity of white maleness. The idealizations of the Noble Savage are important to this construction because they serve to connect the idea of the past to the present by linking modern white men to their past colonial glory through the body of the Indian as a bridge between then and now. The mascot also has most often been represented as a male figure as the frontier was not a place for women of any heritage according to the perspective of these white men.[2] In the contemporary debate over mascots, institutional frameworks are structured to highlight the role of men in these systems and those which have Indian-ness to rely on embolden its persona as a means of public display.

When imagining how masculinity became incorporated into the grounding and use of ideas about Native Americans among the multitude of representations of "Indian-ness" created and constructed around ideas of manliness, manhood, and gender; what the myriad representations have in common is a context of a vacuum that can be thought of as a lack of a coherent model by which to create this desired masculinity. By this I mean that there was nothing of substance about the "American" of which Hector St. John de Crevecoeur queried in 1782 (Deloria 1998:32), it had to be amalgamated and conglomerated, appropriated and constructed, pieced together from bits and pieces of the bodies of representations of masculinity, not unlike a Frankenstein's monster, or, of the scattered multiple reflections of a mosaic of mirrors, by knitting together desired personal reflections of those mirrors. Many disparate pieces were patched together to make the form of the idealized imagined body of men, condensed from the western frontier experiences of the historic American legacy, those that pertain to a degree of masculine importance. When used as a basic form, not unlike a dress maker's pattern or template, Native American constructions were overlain and added to the basic representation to create a wholly new man, combining Eastern and Western hemispheres, Old and New World notions, and Red and White legacies.

White male masculinity, especially as it has been centered on constructed mascot representation and visual imagery at the University of North Dakota, is linked to the Fighting Sioux through constructed tradition of Indian-ness. The Fighting Sioux were dubbed so in 1931, dislocating the current nickname of "Flickertails" to the retired mascots' realm. It is at this site, the UND, which has become the location of the national-level center of the mascot debate. There are many facets of the issue that are represented by the circumstances of the institution, of Native Americans, and of policies that have been convulsively moving along, like an inexperienced driver learning the finesse of a standard transmission automobile, to fits of starts and stops.

The Fighting Sioux nickname and logo has become the current stalwart of mascot resistance in the debate. It has grown and expanded from the university campus to the halls of state government to the national organization of the NCAA. All the while that this debate has ebbed and flowed the interests of the local Sioux communities have been courted for their opinions and favor over the visual and literal namesakes the university's mascot represents. Ideals of white Indian masculinity are embedded in the institution's nickname, one that recalls the efforts of white settlers in trying to claim and tame the prairie landscape and the noble red man foe that stood in the way of this expansion of national borders. White masculinity was evaluated, through the actions of and at the hands of the Indian Fighter, to be superior by the near genocide of the continent's inhabitants; the controlling of the land base of the indigenous inhabitants and its bountiful production by the Farmer Settler; and by the establishment of white male dominance in the course of these actions through the means of ideological national myths and narratives. The idea of the Fighting Sioux as a people, though noble and desired, was also a defeated foe and thus becomes the property of white males as a spoil of victory.

American male identity as it is constructed through masculinity is grounded within fields of nationalism. It is thickly massed around the idea of *American* like muscle. Identity guards it, protects it, and in turn is supported by nationalism like the bone on which the muscle is built up on. This masculinity is exclusive and sees itself as singular in this regard. Abby Ferber contextualizes a critical theory that has revealed the centrality of borders to the construction of coherent identities, the obsession with the process of boundary maintenance which is essential to the construction of race and gender identity (Ferber 1998:6). Control of the issues within manliness asserts a vision of an orderly, property-protecting republic men, set against those Others, those who are the antithesis of a virile and virtuous new American male. Representations of these Others, as oppositional to both "the virtuous republican citizen and the property-owning liberal citizen coded "male," their Others had to be coded "effeminate," or, even worse, as women (Smith-Rosenberg 2010:91). Using manhood as political currency, European Americans embraced a thoroughly racialized sense of masculine self in contrast to the Others. Regarding this nationalism, the American Revolution, established the earliest and most salient context for the invention of a collective European to American identity began when the nation created itself by declaring its independence.

The connection to Native American culture symbolically conveys a return to nature and the embrace of an outdoor life. For example, the Sons of Liberty who adopted Mohawk Indian personas and garb to dump the tea in

Boston Harbor and of the Frontier westerners who identified their own prow-ess and independence within the idealized Indian because they "held similar ideas about Indian character, although their response was one of temporary identification rather than repudiation" (Slotkin 1973:558). The other, more familiar ubiquitous image was that of the savage Indian, the relentless enemy of God and white Americans. In this construction, Native Americans can be presented as creatures of the night, creeping through the wilderness (Smith-Rosenberg 2010:105, 227). This is done to accomplish a sense of habitable space and cultural distance between the two societal groups.

> In the closing years of the nineteenth century, for example, ambition and combativeness became virtues for American men in a new way; competitive-ness and aggression were exalted as ends in themselves. Toughness was ad-mired and tenderness scorned, and perhaps no one embodied these qualities better than President Theodore Roosevelt, whose 1899 speech "The Strenuous Life" called American men to test themselves through adversity. Strength, appearance, and athletic skill mattered more in the Victorian era than in previ-ous centuries. Throughout the twentieth century, American men operated in accordance with these virtues, and they continue to do so today-largely be-cause such notions are a part of our cultural inheritance. (Strain 2010:23)

In 1993, then president of the University of North Dakota Kendall L. Baker issued a public statement on the matter as it sat at that point in time (1993:67). His comments on the matter begin with a reference to an incident at the previous fall semester's Homecoming parade where members of UND's fraternity and sorority system verbally abused a group of Native American youth participating in the activities. Referring to the incident as "unfortunate," he sought to collect as wide a possible range of input from across the state. The state has notoriously been pro-mascot from across the levels of local athletics programs and boosters to government hallways in the state capital. By seeking such input and the time it would have taken to accommodate the views, it seems as he was giving the matter a measure of time to subside and to deflect from the direct issues at hand. This action is similar to that of the University of Illinois and its notorious Garripo intake sessions where a retired judge presided over proceedings at one point of a public forum in which people were given a limited time to air their opinion and a tally of pro- and anti-mascot positions were accounted for and com-piled by the judge. Though he wrote a statement trying to touch on all areas at hand, he decided not to retire the mascot, logo, and nickname and preserve the status quo of white male privilege as his actions bespoke of his acting directly on the matter through nonaction.

Baker back-handedly called attention to the prejudice toward Native Americans at the UND when he commented on the level of racism in his community by claiming that "we need to recognize that this particular incident could have occurred regardless of the nickname we use for our athletic team" (1993:68). This statement also blames the victims for being from a different cultural group. His statement is made more remarkable by the fact that no one at the parade event stood up to help or aid the Native children in any fashion (1993:67). The UND's and the greater Grand Forks area community's disregard for Native Americans was evident through the fact that even children could not register any sympathetic response and support from the viewing public.

Baker further enacts white privilege by claiming that after speaking to "large portions of the broader University community" that was in favor of keeping the Fighting Sioux nickname, he would have to agree with the majority of the UND campus (1993:68). Baker makes his choice of action on the fact that it was made evident to him on a very nearly daily basis since the Homecoming parade and racial harassment incident that the views of Native Americans in attendance at the UND wanted the mascot gone. The small number of Native American student overall in terms of the UND student body would not affect the politics of the campus and its administration, though they would be able to claim a moralist, social justice position in the matter.

Also at issue is that the UND claims to offer a great many educational and academic opportunities for Native Americans at this institution. These claims have the flavor of the boarding school education system in that by the way of educating as many Native American youthful minds, the institution would influence on this population would be great and the Native American youth would be compromised under this system to become a part of American society. How can the UND then justify such academic variety like educations in law, medicine, and education fields as well as the remainder of its curriculum, when it is invested in the maintenance of racialized notions of Indianness as such as the Fighting Sioux?

America and the American man have had a long history of association with the idea of the frontier, of the West. Following along this critical path, masculinity can also be associated with this space/place as well. Susan Lee Johnson views that "the construction of a masculine West was part and parcel of a larger late nineteenth-century 'crisis of manliness' in the United States-a crisis in which older definitions of white, middle-class manhood that emphasized restraint and respectability (manly men) gave way to newer meanings that focused on vigor and raw masculinity (masculine men)" (Johnson 1993:497). In terms of the grounding of these views historically, Carroll Smith-Rosenberg writes "The West helped European Americans, so often troubled and acrimonious, to see themselves as a unique, powerful, and virtuous people—a 'we,' united by collective ownership of the land" (Smith-Rosenberg 2010:207). In creating a manly, rugged independence which is derivative of virtuous American citizenship, implementation of the frontier cowboy myth becomes a centering trope of masculinity. Through the incorporation of the hero icon, America was sitting tall in the saddle, willing to take on all comers, asserting its dominance in world affairs (Kimmel 2012:211), as a white knight acting in a dark world filled with outsiders and others. Jensen connects the past Native American history with that of settlers' colonial history when he remarks that both are real histories and that both histories are "every bit as real as the stories of courageous Norwegian farmers who homesteaded through brutal [Dakota] winters" (2010:35).

Masculinity is a sense of personhood most associated with white men. Maleness is a gendered construct, it is viewed as a condition of biological sex, as a "natural" condition of heterosexuality and social construction that can stand alone. It is part of the make-up of one who doesn't need a (help)mate. This construction of identity uses the Other to make this manifest in the idealization of masculinity as a desired male place. In this identity construct it is inherent "to believe in a protector-provider masculinity whose essential goodness warrants its ongoing right to put and keep the Others in their place" (Pfeil 1995:242). This is placed in opposition to the preferred reading of masculinity primarily represented by Native Americans, especially by grounding it in early American and Colonial time frames. Deloria reviews this process in *Playing Indian* (1998). Heterosexual masculinity embodies personal characteristics such as success and status, toughness and independence, aggressiveness and dominance. These are manifest by adult males through exclusively social relationships with men and primarily sexual relationships with women. In 1972, during the UND's winter festival sponsored by the campus fraternity organizations, one frat house made an ice sculpture of a "topless, Native woman with a sign pointing to her bare breast, saying, 'Lick 'em Sioux'" (Saunders n.d.). A Native American student attending UND protested this display and eventually took an axe to the offending ice sculpture. The ensuing riot between the members of the fraternity and the Native American students protesting the display broke out. At first the only student arrested was the axe-wielding Native American youth. The next day the university president, with advice from AIM, dropped the charges against the lone student and then banned the winter festival as a result. After this confrontation, some fraternity members were quoted in the campus newspaper as saying, "Better dead than red" and "The only good Indian is a dead Indian" (Banks n.d.).

In realizing the changes that were occurring over time in the formation of masculine notions of idealized men and their manhood, most contexts for masculinity, in order to be actualized, revolved around the ability to perform it. This revealed that much of its investment was based upon the receiver's judgment and evaluation upon the individual man's ability to act masculine. Masculinity thus acts like a costume much the same way that mascots are a disguise through its use. "It becomes performative, that is, artificial, calculated, something some men do well, others poorly, some not at all. As a result, which men 'do' masculinity well and which do not is determined, not by the man himself, but by his audience's responses to his performance of manliness" (Smith-Rosenberg 2010:110). [3]

Accordingly, "a man's identity and claim to gendered power derived entirely from his ability to demonstrate hegemonic masculinity" (McCurdy 2011:19). Thomas Foster notes that "historians have shown that in early America successful manhood rested on the establishment of a household, the securing of a calling or career, and the self-control over one's masculine comportment" (Foster 2011:1). He comments further that the conditions of early America affected those norms and ideals of masculinity and linked them to ever-changing regional and nascent American identities (Foster 2011:1). However, masculinity did not remain a static context or category of men's manliness. American cultures changed over time and the values associated with masculinity did as well. This is located in the historic actions of the UND in regard to establishing its Indian identity. In the 1930 school year the name of "Fighting Sioux" is adopted by the campus student body. In that year a booster group formed the Sioux Line Club which helped students paint their faces with "traditional" war paint for home games in order to enact a constructed notion of Indian-ness (Saunders n.d.). In another watershed moment for the UND during the 1930–1931 academic year, the homecoming dance was transformed and became the "First Annual Pow-Wow." This act being another element of the performance and public display of constructed Indian-ness. The problem of performance and public display yielded yet another ugly moment in 1992. During the preparations for the homecoming parade for that year which was when the racial harassment of the Native American youths and adults occurred on the floats in the parade line.

The performance of Indian-ness was taken at issue by the Native American adults on the parade float, and they filed an official complaint of harassment with the UND administration, included the playing of Hollywood-styled Indian music and the mocking display of the "tomahawk chop" (Saunders n.d.). As previously mentioned, nobody from the audience thought this performance of Indian-ness was out of character in regard to the depiction of Native Americans in this college community. It reifies the power embedded in the performance and public display of constructed Indian-ness, especially in the context of whiteness subsuming redness in the preferred modes of playing Indian by the audience.

In the transition of moving from the Colonial and early American ideals expressed in masculinity, American men needed to cling to this foundation of identity as well as to prove that they had become an "improved order of white men." This play on words or notions of definitions from my observation is something that Philip Deloria wrote about in *Playing Indian* (1998) where he noted that white men sought to improve upon Indian-ness through role plays by imagining themselves as being better Indians through such as those actions in the nineteenth century by Lewis Henry Morgan and others by becoming better-than-the-original Red Men (Deloria 1998:58). By white men improving themselves in modernity, remaking themselves to fit into contemporary notions of masculinity, they become their desired ideal, if only through imagined contexts of self.

Another way in which masculinity is performed is through the context of physical or exterior ideals. Here manliness was also defined by physical appearance. To be manly then, "was to be sturdy, healthy, and handsome" in appearance (Syrett 2009:61). Being healthy and robust in one's looks was one way of demonstrating one's masculinity and manliness. In opposition, whiteness as paleness or as pallor can be viewed as one form of weakness as the lack of color and vitality was seen as a detriment to physicality. Penner notes that "the paleface lacks energy and robustness, the paleface lacks masculine vigor" (Penner 2011:5). A suntanned color to the skin meant that this coloration came from being outside, from being active and connected to outdoor activity and such as a good day's labor. This physical occupation lent itself to a strong body and masculine action. Whiteness here is tied to masculinity. Being too white was looked upon as a detriment, of being sheltered and soft. Penner sees this context of whiteness as being too white, effeminate, where a tanned white skin exemplifies action and strength from being outdoors, in contact with the natural world.

This exterior quality is one that is reflective of an active life, a life that was shaped by the natural world and the physical body became strengthened through living in the wilderness. A strong body tempered by contact and conflict with Nature and natural men such as the Indian is robust in color and physical condition. The natural world lends its colorations to the white hero archetype as a sign of a healthy "flush" of tint upon cheek and brow. American heroes combine the elements of the natural world, the physical mettle, and self-reliance of the masculine man, in part answering de Crevecoeur's query.

Richard Slotkin critiques the multiple forms of masculinity and its presentations in historical eras as they are represented through American Heroes. He notes that this archetype symbolizes the masculine ideal as much as it also represents control over the land the hero walks upon. He writes that "the mediating figure of the frontier hero was not only a psychological but a social and political necessity. White Americans required such a figure in order to deal successfully with the Indians in battle, trade, and diplomacy and to live successfully in the wilderness. They also required a moral rationale for claiming and conquering Indian lands" (Slotkin 1973:205). The historic literature helped to lay a foundation for the lone figure of colonialism, for it was believed that wherever the hero stepped could be claimed by the nation in building its possessions. Slotkin notes that the stories and fictions of captivity narratives and dime-store novels told the tales of strife between Native Americans and the European-American interlopers, of the conflicts between his terms of dark races and light, which had formed the basis of the mythology that the Indian fighter and hunter emerged as pre-eminent first national heroes. The fictions and stories myriad authors had "created a character who was to become the archetypal hero of the American frontier, copied by imitators and plagiarists and appearing innumerable times under other names and in other guises-as the man who made the wilderness safe for democracy" (Slotkin 1973:268).

In order for America to become invested in the hero archetype, particularly that of the wilderness hunter, Americans had to accept the ideal as a prototype of masculinity, one which grounds a context for all others to be built upon. The lone hunter ideal was one that relied on independence and individual effort to survive. Slotkin points out that the "acceptance of the hunter as the archetypal American hero meant adopting the hunter's love of exploit and violence for the sake of their blood-stirring excitement" (Slotkin 1973:307). Since this archetype was situated against the backdrop of an encompassing wilderness the literary oppositional of Man against Nature is contextualized. The hero archetype thrives alone in the wild, as a lover of nature and being in that place, and of hunting and surviving, against the representations of nature he finds there as sustenance.

In historical constructions of the hero archetype, many forms of the icon have come into existence. Ranging from the earliest version of the explorer, the naturalist-surveyor, the farmer, the military hero (either a frontier ranger or nationalistic soldier), the white captive raised by the Indian, to the hunter of beasts and men, the hero archetype is adapted to the circumstances of colonialism as it unfolds across North America. In masculine renderings of the archetype, some scholars have advanced lists or categories of the ever-evolving hero. Some authors contend that there are "five traditional archetypes of masculinity—soldier, frontiersman, expert, breadwinner, and lord— [of which they] are now archaic artifacts, although the images remain" (Mishkind et al. 1987:46). Kimmel sees three kinds of male archetypes in use at the turn of the nineteenth century: Genteel Patriarch, a holdover of Euro-Continental aristocracy; the Heroic Artisan, independent, virtuous, honest, partly a holdover in regard to stiff, rigid manners; the Self-Made Man, active in the public sphere, has wealth and status, defined by geographic and social mobility (Kimmel 2012:13).

Here, Smith-Rosenberg refers to the paradox of the white Indian construct in that the wild Indian covered in the evidence of its misdeeds and crimes meets its end at the hands of the hunter archetype whose living beyond civilization in the woods makes him even more violent and deadly than the Indians he pursues and kills. Representing the civilized world, the hunter is drenched in the blood of his own crimes, but his is washed away by his white heritage and the blood goes away to reveal his whiteness of skin and culture. As an engine of destruction and at the same time an agent of civilization, it is necessary for him to wipe out the Redness in order to secure his own White- ness. The frontiersman in the body of "the figure of Daniel Boone, the solitary, Indian-like hunter of the deep woods, that became the most signifi- cant, most emotionally compelling myth-hero of the early republic" (Slotkin 1973:21). Slotkin notes that "the legend of Daniel Boone, whose adventures among the Indians and in the wilderness made him the hero of a nationally achieved viable myth of America. Moreover, it was as a hunter that Boone achieved his heroic stature among Americans" (Slotkin 1973:267).

Another example of this archetype in flux include the "'wild man'; the white man gone native/wild, which could trace back to the mythic history of John Moredock, the white man who lives to kill the Indians who massacred his family, and who lives like an Indian to kill them" (Pfeil 1995:4). The archetype that is most closely associated with the land, the national identity, and independence, reflecting the values embedded in the American Dream is that of the homesteader living on the boundary between savagery and civil- ization. The timeframe of this tenuous existence at the edge of the civilized world lasted from the sixteenth to the end of the nineteenth century, the time of the frontier. It is over this time frame, the solitary uncultured settler eventually transformed into an urban savvy dweller living in the civilized world.

Masculinity is also contextualized by ethnicity in its ideal construction. The hero's whiteness, like its body used as a palimpsest, is inscribed by Otherness in regard to what the hero is ultimately not: he can cross between Red and White worlds, gaining knowledge of the two worlds, but he ends up on the civilized side of the boundary, regaining his civilized persona by wiping the red stains from his body and becoming white again. Susan Lee Johnson notes that "the inevitable white male hero, who is, after all, the true subject of the history of the 'American West'" becomes the default in estab- lishing an historic temporal context to the hero's ideal representation (John- son 1993:495). Slotkin reveals that texts like captivity narratives locate the hero in both worlds and that as an adventurer action-figure "the Indian war narratives developed such a prototype in image of the American soldier-hero as an Indian-like 'hunter'" of Red men (1973:242). [4]

For the white male supporters of the UND Fighting Sioux, the ideal of the hero archetype is internalized by them through the acts of the construction of the Fighting Sioux mascot. For example, the logo design that has been under the most scrutiny in recent times has been the design of Native American artist and UND alumnus, Bennett Brien (Padilla 1999). It is this action by the UND Alumni Association is one that smacks of the paternalism and institu- tionalized racism that harkens back to the processes used in fraudulent treaty making whereby the white man finds a willing individual to affix his "X" mark to paper and in doing so, validating the fraudulent treaty document. In this instance, Brien had been contracted to make several sculptures prior to his painting for Earl Strinden, Alumni Association executive vice president. According to Strinden, Brien had been approached by him privately and commissioned Brien on his own (Padilla 1999).[5] Strinden had noted that Brien's work is "a painting that would give a meaning of pride, heritage, tradition and the strength of character deserving of the Native Americans" (Padilla 1999).

Unpacking the multiple contexts contained within Strinden's rhetoric brings to light several points in the promascot argument of the use and retention of racialized mascots' representations. The "painting" Strinden refers to is a part of the commodification of the idea of the constructed Indian. As an object the painting contains the elements of owning and possessing the image on the canvas, in particular, an Indian through surrogate means of cost and of the evaluation of the Indian corpus for its white possessors. Strinden next states that "meaning" would be added to the quality of possession of the fixed Indian on this canvas, as a culturally appropriated provenance or pedigree to go along with and provided for a history of the object as an art piece. The quality of meaning Strinden speaks of is the fulfilling of the ideals that go into the construction of Indian-ness through popular culture notions. Further, for Strinden, the quality of pride in the image is that of the white man's victory over the Native American where by as a trophy of the conquest of the West the Indian-as-mascot as a controlled commodity contains that pride of success. Heritage refers to the past-to-modern context of cultural history where the Indian is a moment of that history. Tradition refers to the myth of the West and of the Indian who was the human obstacle to that historic chapter. Strinden's idea of the "strength of character" of the constructed Indian is the Noble Savage context of representation. In having the ideal of the Fighting Sioux image realized by a Native American artist, though not of Lakota or Sioux affiliation, the white male supporters of the Fighting Sioux have in hand a real, authentic rendering of the Noble Savage that had become the center point of the UND mascot discourse.

Brien's artwork had become the *de facto* logo for the UND by 1999. Brien, a Chippewa, at first made a painting for a private commission, but its image became so popular among some of the UND community that it was chosen to become the current logo used by the institution. The composition of his work includes a Native American man's face in profile. There is a kinetic appeal to the design in that the man's hair and the feathers attached to the backside crown of his head appear to be blown by a breeze flowing from right to left, from behind the figure to the front. The four feathers are the focal point of the design. Brien notes that such feathers symbolize the accomplishments of any and all students who attend UND, both on a personal and an academic level of achievement (Chmiel 2010). The UND Indian Association, the Native American campus student's group, has stated that though Brien's work is not disrespectful to a Native American audience, the artwork "has not aided the fight against discrimination that still occurs today on [the] UND campus" (UNDIA 2012). Brien commented upon hearing that his creation would be retired by the UND felt that he was "kind of shocked I guess, or kind of sad or whatever. I don't know. I liked it. A lot of people I know liked it" (Chmiel 2010). Brien is academically invested in the UND institution as his father and he himself are graduates of the university, and his son had attended the university, too.

What had garnered the most discourse about Brien's artwork-cum-UND logo are the colors and feathers of the illustration. According to Brien, all aspects of the design are symbolic, especially of the colors within the feathers of the design. "Red was for the blood, feathers for bravery," Brien opined (Chmiel 2010). Red never is actually a part of the feather scheme, it serves as an accent of the face paint for the logo profile. Red is a highlight at the left temple of the face in profile in Brien's work. Yellow and green are a part of the feathers' color scheme. Green is displayed and positioned as a background highlight for the face in profile. Green is also one of the institution colors at UND.

In analyzing the logos that had been employed by the UND over the history of the mascot, I see a connection, perhaps with nostalgia of the UND fan base, between the Brien illustration and to an earlier logo design used as the team's athletics emblem. From 1965 until 1993 the UND had borrowed the team logo of the professional hockey club, the NHL's Chicago Blackhawks for its own hockey team emblem. This logo design had been popular at the UND campus as it was popular and visually recognizable on a much larger public by the use of this version since 1964 by the nationally recognized Chicago Blackhawks hockey team. This heightened the visual public display and visibility of the feathered and painted face and head of Blackhawk, the leader of the Sauk who were located in what would become the state of Illinois. Blackhawk was an opponent of westward United States expansion and he had sided with the British in the War of 1812. In some historical contexts, he was an enemy of the U.S. state.

Today, this image of Blackhawk is coveted in some parts of the nation as much as it is recognizable in relation with professional sports. The image of the formerly Ignoble, now considered as a Noble Savage, Blackhawk-the-Enemy has now become Blackhawk-the-Commodity. It is this quality of visibility that the UND was able to achieve by the use of such a visible quantity as the Chicago hockey club logo. The Brien version can be compared for content of the image to that of the Chicago hockey logo.

The first example of similar content is the Noble Savage. The images convey a sense of visual focus as well as a slight smile by the Brien version and one of ease or trust by the Chicago version which has a slight smile, too.

The Noble Savage is raised here in the example of the two countenances of the images. In the construction of the romanticized Noble Savage, a desired male figure of some particular trait or strength becomes the ideal on which the two logos can be grounded. The Noble Savage is a help-mate to the white man, and is a trusted sidekick at closest contact. As well, the Noble Savage is a stoic, a brave face in the on-coming unrolling carpet of Western civilization. The Brien version seems full of emotion, yet the pursed lips keep the head silent.

A second example is that of the glossy black hair on both profiled faces. The black color of the hair is contextualized as a means of ethnic, racial, or cultural identity. The hair in the Chicago logo is a racializing marker of identity since its inception in 1926. It was also in this year that the University of Illinois adopted a white male student as a constructed Indian as its mascot, Chief Illiniwek. This version of constructed Indian-ness by the university was wildly successful in its acceptance and adoption by the institution. In this popular culture era of America, Native Americans were becoming more and more represented as sports team logos and nicknames. The successes of the Carlisle Indians or the Oorang Indians were still a recent memory. Thus, long hair as an accessory of constructed Indian-ness of this mimicked ethnicity becomes one way in order to identify the Indian male. The white males accept the gender of the ideal, but not necessarily the personality of it.

A third example is that both illustrations face to the left of the observer, showing the face in profile. This may seem an either/or placement as to the position of the drawings, facing left or right in the compositions. But with both the older rendition of the Chicago version and the more recent Brien version, I see a connection between the logos in this positioning of the faces in profile.

A fourth example is of the feathers which adorn the two versions of Indian maleness. As Brien had noted, feathers are symbols of accomplishment and deed. The feathers seem to the most recognizable accessory of Indian-ness associated with the popular notions of it. It seems to that to add feathers to any representation makes it more ethnic and calls to mind Indian-ness. Feathered Native American representations have been a part of the European version of Indians from initial contact. This is in part of the aesthetic and symbolic meanings embedded in feathers. Some were worn by cultural and social elites in some societies. Some were gendered in context as men of social or religious or military fraternities awarded feathers as markers of accomplishment and status to their members. Feathers were used for the recognition of personal conduct and role model behaviors that were desired by the particular community conferring such accords. The use and acceptance of both logos of Indian men in profile captures the audience imagination where the Noble Savage helps to reify white male masculinity through a visual representation of Native American men.

The Chicago Blackhawks asked the UND to stop using the logo in 1993. Brien's version of the logo design was retired at the start of the 2012–2013 academic year. Today, the UND has moved on to a geometric-style of interlocking capital letters "N" and "D" design as its logo. It is illustrated in green, black, and white, the UND's school colors.

Brien's artwork serves an example of white masculinity being inscribed upon a red identity. The construction of Indian-ness as represented by the painting by Brien which became the logo used by the UND symbolizes the cultural appropriation of an Indian ethnic notion by way of Brien, a Chippewa, creating the image for a white alumni booster of the university. The artwork then was gifted to the UND by Strinden. The image, in turn, caused such excitement in the belief that Strinden's art piece was the new logo for the university that the weight of the conversation on campus pushed it along in that direction (Padilla 1999). Through the use of another example of identity construction at the UND, the circumstances surrounding the donation of a gift of a privately funded ice hockey venue by an alumnus became entangled with the mascot controversy. Ralph Engelstad, along with the ice arena he built for the UND, also became a center-piece of the discourse. This particular situation was reflective of the construction of whiteness as it had been accessorized by Sioux redness within the building of the hockey rink on the UND campus. This also came to represent the most contentious of matters in the debate over the use of mascots, nicknames, and logos associated with the UND.

In the construction of a hockey arena that reflects the construction of white masculinity which had appropriated idealized Indian imagery, this sports venue extensively used the Brien image as a decorative element in the making of the ice rink. The ice arena represented in its contentious construction equal parts of money as a funding resource, the influential power of that money; the ego of the alumnus spending the cash on the project, the vanity of the donor as a private entrepreneur; and race for the construction of the arena challenged all elements of the mascot discourse both from within and from without the institution infrastructure (Brownstein 2001:46–49).

Engelstad had had a checkered past as an actor in this contention over the ice hockey arena and the mascot controversy. In his college days at UND, he had been a goaltender for the hockey team for one season. After his college days were over, he went on to Las Vegas where as a business entrepreneur he operated two casinos, one in Las Vegas, the other in Mississippi, and began to make a personal fortune for himself. It is during this period that Engelstad became notorious for his behavior and his political leanings. At one of his casinos, he had celebrated Adolph Hitler's birthday, throwing a party to mark the occasion. Also, he had dressed in German World War II regalia for these events. He even had bumper stickers made saying, "Hitler was right." The

Nevada gaming commission fined him $1.5 million for such behavior in 1989.

In 1998, Engelstad approached the UND with a proposition to donate and build an ice hockey arena. His $104 million dollar donation is the largest given to the UND. The arena was completed and opened for its inaugural game against the Boston University Terriers in 2001. However, the path to this event was not without complications for Engelstad, the UND, or the Sioux/Lakota people both on and off campus.

Engelstad's approach to the institution happened during the height of the contentious debate over mascots at the UND. Because of the contentious argument and the attention the discourse was receiving from the national level of mascot debate where the UND was now attaining the position on par with the "most resistant site" as it was then held by the University of Illinois, Engelstad began to play a game of "chicken" with the UND. He threatened to rescind his donation of a hockey arena, and leave the bulk of the project unfinished and let it rust in the North Dakota climate. He did so by sending a letter of his intention to then UND president Kupchella, outlining his threat and his ransom for his continued funding of the arena project (Engelstad in *The Chronicle of Higher Education* 2001:47). His demands included that the UND keep the name of the Fighting Sioux for the life of the arena; the UND was to keep the Brien artwork-as-logo as an ubiquitous feature of the arena décor; and the arena would be privately held by the Engelstad family who would thus maintain control over the facility in order to keep the "Fighting Sioux" name and logo as requirements in order to complete the building project even as it was built upon UND campus grounds. Engelstad stated that he willing to take a $35 million loss of the unfinished project in order to get his way (Engelstad in *The Chronicle of Higher Education* 2001:47). Another part of Engelstad's play was the co-construction of a basketball and volley-ball court space with the same demands for décor and ownership control. As a result of the construction of the two athletics sites, the hockey venue was dubbed "The Ralph" as the moniker of the Ralph Engelstad Arena, and the basketball/volleyball facility known colloquially as "The Betty" for the Betty Engelstad Sioux Center. The UND disregarded the concerns of Native American students attending the university by opting for athletics and eco-nomic prestige rather than for social justice and an open academic environ-ment and reputation for all students of any stripe.

The result of Engelstad's letter was a complete reversal of institution policy. Weeks before Engelstad's ransoming of the building project, the UND had voted to retire the logo. One day after Engelstad's letter was made public to Kupchella et al, the UND rescinded and reversed its intended policy to retire the mascot and caved to Engelstad's demands of keeping the nick-name and logo. The commission board chosen by Kupchella to study the naming controversy voted 8–0 in favor of keeping the logo, nickname, and mascot intact (Brownstein 2001:47). The UND thus reified its position as a bastion of racism and as a fortress of white privilege by its actions. The Native American education programs and opportunities the UND had touted in response to the allegations of hypocrisy and the disregard of Native American concerns was once again shown as a hollow claim and as a façade of its own institutional racism against Native American people. The rhetoric of honoring Native Americans by the use of the word "fighting" and the constructed imagery of idealized Indian-ness were realized as flaccid excuses in the light of this particular contention of mascot discourse.

Ralph Engelstad passed away in 2002. But prior to his passing, "The Ralph" opened in 2001. In the construction of the shrine to his own personification of his masculinity, Engelstad made use of the Brien artwork to an unprecedented degree. Both inside and outside of the hockey arena, Engelstad made nearly unlimited use of the Fighting Sioux logo. A granite floor logo was placed in the entrance to the arena. The end of each aisle of seats had the logo as an endcap for the rows. The utility carpet contained the logo. The steps of the stairs in the arena had the logo on them, too. Also, he had a larger-than-life-size bronze statue made of his self which was placed at the main entrance of the arena, located across from the doorway, and stood superior to the Brien logo, above the disembodied head of the granite logo. [6] He had been able to do this because of the way he had negotiated the agreement between him and the UND. As a privately controlled and owned facility, the Engelstad family retained the control over the decorating of the arena. In order to combat the movement to retire the Brien logo, Engelstad wanted to make the logo as ubiquitous as possible, and if the retirement of the logo should happen, he wanted to make the removal of the over two thousand logos as unappealing and as expensive a task as possible. He had done this to spite those who wished to end the UND connection to the visual imagery of Sioux masculinity, the disembodied head of the Brien logo of the Fighting Sioux mascot.

The nickname "Fighting Sioux" was in large letters on the outside of the building as well as a bronze of Lakota leader Sitting Bull astride a horse that welcomed the visitors and fans to the arena. Another Fighting Sioux logo carved into a medallion was attached to the wall near the main entrance and was plainly visible to all who walked by into the arena. Similar decorating was done to The Betty, also. This included the logo being painted onto the court floor, as well as being imprinted on the seats' fabric and cushions.

The Ralph Engelstad Arena was constructed as a monument to the self as a function of ego, and also done in order to confound the anti-mascot agenda of social justice of the mascot debate. The arena had become a testament to the "most resistant" of discursive sites in the mascot debate. This had been, I argue, held formerly by the University of Illinois. The UI institution's former position against the retirement of its mascot, Chief Illiniwek, marked it as so.

Now, the UND had positioned itself as the site of pro-mascot stalwart. With The Ralph serving as a frame or backbone for the construction of white male masculinity guised as Native American ideal, the arena, the UND, and the Lakota people of North Dakota are entwined in a boondoggle that has yet to be fully reconciled to any side's satisfaction. As long as the arena is privately controlled by the Engelstad family who favors the use of the mascot, logo, and nickname, there will certainly be an undercurrent of tension and racialization as a subtext of the mascot discourse on campus, and as the most public of contentious sites in the national level of debate on racialized mascots.

The mascot controversy had not been limited to the UND campus (where in April 2010 the UND decided once again to drop the mascot either as two communities of Lakota, the Spirit Lake and Standing Rock Sioux tribes, were at odds in terms of supporting the mascot or not) (Barrett 2010).[7] One community, the Spirit Lake Sioux Nation has been supportive of the retention of the mascot, logo, and nickname, particularly the nickname, Fighting Sioux (Florio Internet:2010). The Standing Rock community had yet to resolve the issue (Barrett 2010). In 2009, the Spirit Lake community had filed a law suit to keep the Fighting Sioux nickname because the nickname and the recognition by the public of the people it is named for is a source of "honor and worry that abandoning it would send them one step closer to obscurity" (Davey 2009:A18). One Spirit Lake community member had said that an end to the nickname would not soothe relations between white North Dakotans and American Indians, whether on the UND campus or off. Of such actions and racialized histories of the region one publication interviewee commented that the UND is not the Deep South (Brownstein 2001:47). In light of the controversies surrounding the mascot contention and the just-below-the-surface racism here in this space, it is located, rather, in the Deep North.

In the various acts of denial by the mascot supporters, it is the denial of the harm that it does to Native Americans on the whole which is paralleled by the denial of their own humanity. As a result, as long as the name of "Fighting Sioux" remains in place, it will continue to foster an atmosphere of potential racialized harassment of Native American students on campus. In order to affirm their own humanity, the Euro-American must acknowledge that quality in indigenous people.

In constructing iconic Indian-ness around masculine ideals of white males, the invented Indian is manipulated like a pose-able doll that can be contorted into any desired position or shape. The forms that the constructed Indian assumes reflect both the desired and undesired aspects of white masculinity. For example, as the constructed Indian is emulated for being brave and strong, it is contradicted by perceptions of the Indian as being sneaky and treacherous. It is the latter two characterizations of the Indian which must be negated by white masculine colonial actions. Even as masculinity is defined and grounded through the idealized Indian, notions of race, ethnicity, and culture permeate the construction of the white male via the Indian male. White thus becomes the over-riding superstructure on which the ideal Indian is stretched and made to cover. The undergirding of whiteness then becomes the main body on which Indian-ness is constructed in this context of mascot representations.

Chapter Three

White Identity, White Ideologies, and Conditions of Whiteness

The Seneca youth who performed the act of the Noble Savage in the school gymnasium played a role that fit the scripted notions of the performance of Indian-ness, these notions derived from stereotypes and expectations of what an Indian is and how it behaves. These notions, stereotypes, and expectations are ideas which are held by mainstream Americans because they are grounded collective American popular culture which makes things Indian an object. As a symbolically white-derived populace, America uses Whiteness as a mirror to determine its favored readings of Indian-ness. These elements were combined and publically displayed by the Seneca teenager. The costume of the young man had the requisite long feathered headdress, the tomahawk, moccasins, fringed clothing, and stoic demeanor. The white members of the audience saw what they desired in terms of the ideal constructed Indian body. The white color of the leather outfit worn by the young Seneca man was unmarred by stain or color; thus, it symbolically reflected back whiteness.

Whiteness, and the contributing dimensions of it, is connected to the idealized notion of the Native American–based mascots as a construct with which it is used to locate difference, both physically and socioculturally, between Native Americans and native-born Americans. The idea of whiteness informs these social and physical parameters to create a condition of difference which is used by the white mainstream to validate ideas of power and privilege against and over Native American peoples. The use of physical differences between groups of people in order to distinguish one group from another is one function of the process that has had racialized and ethnocized contexts attached to its application in regards to colonialized people.

By constructing an evaluated system like physical differences as a marker, a hierarchical categorization construct becomes grounded, one which places values on skin color, hair texture, and facial features among other similar items as criteria. In constructing whiteness using "race" as the valuating principle, these criteria define whiteness for what it is and what it is not in relation to those other groups. This is accomplished through the idea that whiteness is a global factor that is located within the hegemonic ideals of the West and applied as a cultural influence world-wide. Following behind the mechanisms of colonialism, the West has become a cultural transporter to places outside of the scope of the continental United States or of the European continent, too. In 1998, the American Anthropological Association (AAA) published a statement on the use of the idea and construction of race as a socially engendered operational practice which has no basis in human biology. The AAA concluded that this idealization of race as a legitimate item was created in order to continue the forms of power that perpetuate social, economic, and spatial differences. [1] Also, the ideas of difference used as constructions of race are transportable. Richard Drinnon writes of this process in his work, *Facing West: The Metaphysics of Indian-Hating and Empire-Building* (1980). He observes that as colonial empire of the West/ Europe/America expanded beyond its home territorial boundaries, the processes and mechanisms of colonialism went along as a sidekick to this action. Since the Western/American version that was founded within in its own political geographic bounds was based in North America, its subjects of colonialism were the "Indians" of the frontiers of these lands. Drinnon points out that as American empire began to expand beyond its continental borders into the Pacific Rim, these new frontiers of "the West," located now in lands and peoples of the Pacific Ocean region, the idea of the Indian Other became part of the overall process which travelled along with this expansion. From this perspective of colonialism, Hawaiians, Philippine Islanders, Samoans, and more Pacific peoples became the new localized "Indians," now encountered on a global stage.

In constructing whiteness, there are multiple facets which have been used to construct the notions of it as a social device, couched in forms of power. Whiteness, the qualities of being white, and the meanings associated with it as a color or hue, and the ideological properties of it as a race of people, has many parameters of it as a subject matter. White maintains a position of power through the multiple contexts of its constructed complexity. It is in this scope that hierarchies of difference have come about from the groundings of whiteness, with some of these ideas based in social, cultural, economic, and ideological frames. White and all that it engenders in this discussion is a construct which is dependent upon the Indian-as-mascot as a reflective component of identity. In the above mentioned binaries in which Redness and Whiteness are compared and contrasted, the binaries point to positive and negative characteristics of Redness which is evaluated by Whiteness. This context in terms of race and ethnicity is one where the mascot is a trophy of white colonialism, and is a symbol, as well as a physical, animate entity which points to the differences between the two groups, which the racialized mascot role plays on the sidelines for the viewing audience. In portraying the antics of expected Indian behavior whilst taking cues from the consuming white public audience in regard to the reactions of their emotional involvement in viewing a sporting contest, the mascot plays Indian for the public gaze; it performs this spectacle of ethnic display for public consumption.

The Native American then represents a reality which is not in the purview of the mascot's constructed "authenticity" whereby the "real Indians" face much different circumstances in their own communities both on and off the reservation, and away from the gaze of the mainstream public world. Mascots represent a different, constructed reality in which whiteness becomes legitimized by creating Native American-based mascots which are then used to gloss over the lethal history of North American colonialism. This is accomplished by the ability to suspend sense and reason about this part of the national history of America because now, the Indian-as-mascot is "safe" and tamed, dancing on the sidelines, performing to the conqueror's drumbeat. As well the masquerader whom is performing Indian-ness on the sidelines is most likely a white male student chosen to have the honor of role playing "Indian" during these public performances of Indian-ness.[2] Black discusses this presumed cultural identity conundrum as an alumnus of such an institution of higher learning which uses a Native American–based mascot (2002:605). Though he is not a member of a tribal entity, one is given to him, conferred onto him as a graduate, especially when the institution is seeking donations for its fundraising efforts he retorts.

Another facet of this ability or power to play Indian is the setting for the viewing audience's location. As part of a college campus or secondary school site, the performances are done under the eye of the academic institution, acting as a legitimizing agent because of the authority given to this socio-cultural agent by the mainstream. Because the role plays are performed on a setting which lends itself to the purpose of education and the dissemination of factual information for the public, the idea of the stereotypic Indian gains an aura of authenticity by the setting of the presentation for public consumption. And, since this may be the only time that many members of the audience will ever meet a "real, live Indian" on display this experience could well be the only time that a context is given to Native Americans outside of American history and its texts. Mascots, then, serve whiteness as a measurement of civilized society, and of the success of the colonial enterprise becoming utilized as a living symbol of the conquered and tamed lands and peoples. Native Americans become submerged in the public view and as represented by mascots are more readily available to the mainstream popular culture as an historic figure that represents a conquered and colonized group which lost the battle for land in regard to the nation-building enterprise of the Euro-colonial settlers in establishing their country. It is within these contexts that whiteness is grounded and legitimized by the use of the mascot to rationalize and glorify the dispossession and dislocation of the Native American peoples of North America.

In constructing mascots around ideals of whiteness, it comes into two of the four areas mentioned by C. Richard King as problematic areas of research when studying anthropology and sports, that of context (authenticity) and people (others) (2004:31). It appears that white people are authentic as are the mascots of constructed Indian-ness, which are based on real Native Americans who are considered not to be inauthentic, and further, that white-ness confers personhood upon those who are white while those who are not white are the Others. It is in this vein that constructed mascots reflect notions of identity that reflect what is and what is not white as well as notions of reality in which white racism is accepted, particularly in commercial contexts of production (King and Springwood 2001:87–89). From within the acade-my, the connections between anthropology and sports are considered at best "illegitimate, questionable, and marginal" (King 2004:31).

This particular quality of mascot portrayal is best exemplified by the Florida State University Seminoles. Its mascot version presentation is a near-ly silent, stoic presentation of Indian-ness. Save for a single war-whoop during the display or spectacle made during the opening events for home football games, the contemporary mascot's posings are of the stoic, crossed-arms variety (King and Springwood 2001:83). However, such behaviors are often exhibited in the stands by the audience, the predominantly white view-ers of the FSU sports contests. Whiteness is reified by the use of the symbol of Native American resistance, Chief Osceola, however now defeated and, after being decapitated, with his head a trophy which is symbolic of American military prowess; in the "Tomahawk Chop," the burlesque of In-dian modes of trophy collection as a scalp-hunting process; the sports booster group, the Scalphunters; and the myriad forms of body-painting, approxima-tions of Indian dances, and be-feathered accessories that tell of authentic Indian-ness to this crowd. The crowd's actions are quite possibly linked to the idea by some scholars that the Everglades, the home of the Seminoles, and by larger context, the state of Florida, was once presented as the last frontier, a dislocated pre-Wild West with its own resident wild people (Mechling 1998:152).

Hegemonic masculinity is built upon contexts of racism and racist prac-tices. The exclusion of Redness in order to locate Whiteness means the expunging of it so that what is left then becomes whitewashed and thus serves as a base for the inscriptions and colorings of the hues of whiteness upon the covered over canvas. Laurel Davis has observed that men of color still occupy a back seat relative to white men, in the hierarchy of masculinities, as the hegemonic masculine subject is defined as the white man (1997:96). Reified through leisure activities that have been dominated by strength, competition, violence, and achievement in this public sphere are exclusive to men. This idea and setting promotes a societal ideal of a public masculinity that encompasses play and games as sport that is glorified through white men's participation and success. In glorifying whiteness, the use of Native American-based mascots is the most common representations of sports teams. Animals are the second most popular representation. Both have aggressive and lethal contexts associated with their respective portrayals, and both are considered inhuman. Linking Native Americans with animals degrades the human and makes them bestial in their qualities.

Mascots in terms of their use and forms of power embedded within them "reflect and reinforce a model of [a] contemporary version of colonialism: symbolic colonialism. The hegemonic masculine subject is a symbolic colonizer" (Davis 1997:116). Mascots are at their base or core are anti-Native American, though they are touted as honoring of their memory and with "no disrespect intended" toward Native peoples in the defensive rhetoric of them. Mascots are necessarily created by non-Native Americans as idealized notions of what constructed Indian-ness is all about in their mind's eye. As a mode or signifier of difference and of desired ideals, mascots are based on racialized stereotypes of Native American peoples and cultures. The anti-flavor of the construct reveals the inherent perspective of racial superiority of whiteness.

This attitude incorporates colonial and imperial contexts of difference that are not just skin deep, and many notions go to the bone. Difference as presented in the mascot construction include degrees of nudity as clothing has become a marker of civilization and culture; lethality as the mascot often is armed to some degree by tomahawk, knife, lance, or war club; associations with primitive and wild accessories like bird feathers, animal skins or pelts, bone or claw adornments, natural pigments or colorings on the body; and skin color as the deeper the red shade of the skin the deeper the context of wildness is set in the stereotype of the Indian. Scholars point to the end of the nineteenth century as a time when whiteness was in crisis for white males as industrialization, the closing of the frontier, the end of the Indian Wars, and the rise of urban life as a feminizing criterion in America. Frederick Jackson Turner locates the year 1890 as this turning point in white male tensions.

In these terms, whiteness as a normative context is condensed through the mascot of derivation of Seminole manliness, Osceola, at the Florida State University. C. Richard King has noted that "although Chief Osceola does portray a historic war leader of the Seminoles, he defines Indianness solely in terms of aggressiveness, savagery, and violence" (2010:150). These attributes are then glossed over as to not represent real Native American people but rather the fantastic, fictionalized constructs that are the embodiments of these behaviors to the white beholder. The appropriations of Indian-ness then become the property of its creators, the white audience of supporters and viewers. These conventions done for the benefit of whiteness serve claims for white appropriation and their self-worth. The contrived Indian becomes "theirs." Thus, these symbols, as silent yet loaded visual language, help frame what whiteness is and is not.[3]

One example of this is the "tomahawk chop" of FSU fan origin. Former university president Dale W. Lick commented in 1993 that the tradition began from fan participation, not something from within the university, and it is not part of the sanctioned, official activities which surround FSU Semi-nole-ness (King 2010:153). As an institutional tradition, the "chop" seems readily prepared for use from right off the Hollywood soundstage as a theat-rical embellishment of stereotypic Indian behavior.

Institutional racism is also a part in the arguments for mascot retention as whiteness has glossed over redness in the power of representation that occurs when the sideline Indian performs in public. In some instances of pro-mascot retention circumstances, Native Americans themselves have condoned and supported such practices. In the FSU case, the Seminole Nation of Florida had in the past endorsed the mascot charade. By doing so, the Seminole Nation gets publicity from this relationship and the successes of the athletics program at FSU helps in gaining this notoriety. King observes that this relationship smacks of the legacy of treaty-making to "legitimate imperial actions" by using select Native Americans to endorse such things (2010:156). In this realm of sport, white male behavior of violence was interconnected with order to produce a paradox of ideals engendered in mas-cots as a representation of the wild with the tamed, the good with the bad, the hostile coupled with the friendly, all varieties of the Indian in one collective frame.

In combining white racial superiority with that of education institutional commercialism, the Seminoles of Florida and FSU Seminoles are entered in a symbiotic relationship where white racism is allowed while Native American visibility is gained. Both sides benefit from this relationship of publicity and compromise. In regard to the context of race and racism, in American contexts of it, a flattened definition of it has defined it as either black or white in its comparisons. Native Americans as red-skinned people are neither black nor white and that because of this distinction as defined by a white racial dynamic context, they fall out of the parameters of that definition of what I call "American 'classic' racism." By this logic, mascots are not racist in their nature because they are not historically or culturally black in their public presentations. The mascots invoke another kind of cultural guilt in regard to the past treatment of Native Americans. As Barbara E. Munson has noted, "as long as such logos[, nicknames, and mascots] remain, both Native American and non-Indian children are learning to tolerate racism in our schools" (2010:13).

The use of postcolonial critique in the framework to evaluate the resistance to end mascot portrayals provides for a lens from which to review the claims of the pro-mascot camp. This group justifies such presentations of Indian-ness as a tradition, as rhetoric of privilege, and as a consolidation of white-ness that is grounded in colonial historical lingerings as a form of power. This resistance has been detailed throughout the protest against mascots by Native Americans and their supporters over the years as represented by Dart-mouth Indians, Stanford Indians/Prince Lightfoot, Syracuse Orangemen/Sal-tine Warrior, Illinois Fighting Illini/Chief Illiniwek, North Dakota Fighting Sioux/Sitting Bull, and the Florida State Seminoles/Osceola. The use of mas-cots here is predominantly in the semiotic context of their meanings. As symbols of the constructed Other, mascots incorporate power, conquest, leg-acy, national identity, and control of colonized peoples. The visual language of images, though silent in nature, speaks loudly through the ideas it conjures in the viewer's mind's eye. This is a powerful process in that the images viewed are brought back from the past as memory and into the present, tied with an emotional context, becomes a form of nostalgia that is a potent mixture of past and present. In the case of the Florida State University Semi-noles, the cultural memory of the white fan base sees themselves as glorious fighters and historic markers of independent resistance. Crossing this mental image is the notion of pageantry and ceremony associated with Indian-ness. Yet undergirding these two veins is that of colonial privilege which makes Indians subjects of mimesis and alterity. This constructed ethnic identity is thus political and economically profitable that defines a boundary between red and white. In this mechanism, whiteness consumes Indian-ness while together they erase redness and Native-ness from the public's cultural eye.

It becomes at some point in the debate an institutional matter. In this instance, the institution becomes the advocate for Native Americans in pro-ducing a policy that would protect Native Americans from such cultural practices, defending from such educational institutions like the Florida State University or University of North Dakota or Eastern Michigan University (formerly) Hurons (*Indian Country Today* 2012). With such institutions like education and government supporting such practices, racism becomes a pub-lic institution such as the two represent. Staurowsky writes of a "cultural illiteracy" in terms of institutional knowledge in regards to Native American history in the Western hemisphere. She points out that the lack of basic cultural literacy the process or mechanism for delivery of more broadly con-ceived and of a truer reading of indigenous contributions and inventions (2010:65). This knowledge if correctly dispersed in its mission of educating its intended white male audience would produce a more informed cultural awareness and literacy in the lives of Othered peoples. Without this, the cultural illiteracy of this part of the American public would remain elevated. This would further the conditions of the dysfunction she says of this ideal delivery form as long as white male Americans thought of Native Americans naively-considered and objectified gaze (Staurowsky 2010).

Since this cultural literacy, or the lack of it, is just one aspect of failure by the education institutions in the evaluating of the conditions and worth of Native American and indigenous peoples in North America for their own audience's knowledge. By having an advocate like a supervisory or official governing body such as the NCAA, making policy to protect Native Americans' civil rights, such actions would set the slow movement of cultural perception in motion, with the end of such mascots by several generations' time and passing. Staurowsky locates the lack of a truer perspective of Native American people as a condition of the lack of culturally relevant knowledge as result of the dysfunction of its delivery system (2010:65). What this lack of cultural literacy reinforces are the norms established by whiteness ranging from privilege, practices, and forms of the content of whiteness. She notes further in these conditions that American capitalist consumer culture does not encourage racial sensitivity (2010:72).

This contention had lead scholars such as Lawrence Baca to ask, "[Why] white folks just don't get it?" (2010:80). It is the processes of power and privilege that combine to negate the moralist context of questions over social justice from the perspective of the mascot supporters. In the past studies of this phenomenon critical race theory has provided for some tools to critique the positions of whites and whiteness. It also highlights yet another paradox in mascot contentions, that of progressive policies adopted by institutions and their governing bodies along with providing the space for continued status quo of mascot portrayals. In the case of the Florida State University, it is the acceptance and approval by the Florida Seminoles of the university to use such presentations of Indian-ness while the NCAA policy waffles through its own intentions by letting FSU continue to use the iconography of Osceola as its representative Indian when it has stated that such portrayals must end (Castagno and Lee 2010:89; Harjo 2010:180; NCAA 2005). Such institutional actions fall short in upholding social justice as a policy priority.

A facet of this contention is the potential influence of past students, as alumni who contribute to their alma mater. Potential harm through the lack of their collective non-giving is played upon as a reason not to give up and retire Native American–based mascots. The reason is tied to the nostalgic experience of the alumni concerned that the retirement of the college's Indian mascot would not provide the same experience for current and future students (McEwan and Belfielf 2010:128). This potential loss threatens those memories and possibly revenue for the institution. Through the acts of alumni-giving and revenue stream, the institution is given a trump card to play in the debate.

However, decisions made about racially-derived mascots will mark those institutions that do not retire them. It is a telling action which calls into question the legacy of its institutional stand on social justice. McEwan and Belfielf find, in general, that the impacts of alumni not committing to donations will be minimal and that bachelor's-degree-granting-only institutions suffer only a slight decline from a small percentage of alumni donors not committing to fund-raising pledges (2010:128). Wahlberg notes that in reviewing 27 institutions that did undergo name changes that in five-year periods before and after name changes that there was no discernible loss of fans and, by extension, fan dollars after the mascot identity change (2010:124). Others, though, see the changes made by some institutions to retire such mascots as a trend, glacially moving it may seem, as it has gone on for over forty years, of the outcome for the eventual end of such displays that produce conflict rather than unity on universities with racialized mascots.

There are multiple contexts and applications of the concept of white. The color of white glosses over all other colors to leave a blankness of nothingness that becomes an over-riding effect, which becomes the reality of space. "Many works on whiteness call for recognition of the ways in which whiteness serves as a sort of invisible norm, the unraced center of a racialized world" (Newitz and Wray 1997:3). Whiteness is everywhere in American culture, but it is very hard to locate and pin down in terms of its visibility. As the unmarked category against which difference is constructed, "whiteness never has to speak its name, never has to acknowledge its role as an organizing principle in social and cultural relations" (Lipsitz 1998:1). White can be a political statement or process that is exclusive as it is overemphasizing its own properties of self and conceptualization. In another construct, white becomes ubiquitous as an either/or representation of "normal" or accepted. As such, it can viewed as a leveler, yet in paradox, it is as a context of something that is perceived of as better than that to which it is being compared. In this structure whiteness has physical, psychological, political, and economic factors which support its self-actualizations while creating spaces that show where it is lacking, places where it is not white.

Whiteness serves as an assimilation mechanism. Whiteness does this as it overlays the contours of the discourse on racialized mascots by the act of it assuming a position of authority via its standing as an education institution. In this case, academic institutions like colleges and universities which have such portrayals of Native Americans see themselves as such because they are places of higher learning. Pewewardy notes that the use of mascots and the impact of them upon Native American youth plays "a crucial role in the distorting and warping American Indian children's cultural perceptions of themselves, as well as non-Indian children's attitude toward and simplistic understanding of American Indian culture" (2004:181). By being an "authority" on the matter as an academic stakes holder, their judgments become accepted by the non-Native viewer through the use of academic-couched power as a social observer and evaluator on the issue. In other words, whiteness judges itself and those things around it. In terms of the dual identities surrounding the FSU Seminoles, such an identity complex is grounded through paradoxical means.

Non-Native fans and supporters of FSU sports are conferred a Native American Indian-ness by their association with the sports team where the dual identities of redness and whiteness are overlapped with one another in order to produce white Indians on the sidelines and in the stands and bleachers. The color of whiteness, of being white, glosses over all other colors to leave a blankness of nothingness that becomes an over-riding effect, which in turn becomes the reality of space. "Many works on whiteness call for recognition of the ways in which whiteness serves as a sort of invisible norm, the unraced center of a racialized world" (Newitz and Wray 1997:3).

Whiteness is everywhere in American culture, but it is very hard to locate and pin down in terms of its visibility. As the unmarked category against which difference is constructed, "whiteness never has to speak its name, never has to acknowledge its role as an organizing principle in social and cultural relations" (Lipsitz 1998:1). White can be a political statement or process that is exclusive as it is over-emphasizing its own properties of self and conceptualization. In another construct, white becomes ubiquitous as an either-or representation of "normal" or accepted. As such, it can viewed as a leveler, yet in paradox, it is as a context of something that is perceived of as better than that to which it is being compared. In short, whiteness makes for better Indians, real or imagined.

The first use of the word white as a racial definition was in 1604. This locates the use of the word in the American colonies in the seventeenth century. Beginning in the seventeenth century, social elites did not see themselves as physically white, as they were still imagining that "the word 'white' had uses as a noun" (Roediger 2008:1). As the American legacy of colonization shows, settlers made themselves white out of the process of dispossessing the Native Americans, though how they did it through violence becomes a black-and-white memory of the dispossession of lands. In order to accommodate this view, whites often cast themselves as the victims of Indian aggressions, done to prove that they were civilized and justified in violence against the Indian. This then led to the physical attacks on the Native Americans by acting on the belief that such attacks protected white's property. In this context, individualized possession and personally-held property equals white.

In the Western society white is accepted as the norm for society and for people. For most whites, skin color is not an issue. It does not involve a sense of consciousness as it pertains to social status because it is not a part of their social standing. In equating the idea of being white with being human secures for them a position of power. White people naturally have this power and believe that they think, feel, and act like and for all people. White people create the dominant images of the world in their own image: white people set the standards of humanity by which they are bound to succeed and others are bound to fail (Dyer 1997:9). They have tended to see themselves as racially invisible. Whites are said to consider themselves a neutral universal category, hence non-racial and superior to "racialized" others. "Their self-image as whites is thus both underdeveloped and yet extremely presumptuous" (Newitz 1997:132).

In regard to the imagined Seminoles, whiteness allows only for the constructed to become real, that the real Seminoles as a business partner with FSU are still only backdrop material, still only two-dimensional like movie props. The real Seminoles in this context, then, are as real as the use of them in this relationship allows them to be. They are thought of as distant and out of place though they are peers of the FSU institution in one relationship. The consumptive aspect of this red-white binary reflects the white hegemonic control over the Native American body.

As a result, during the transitional period from Colonial times to modernity, in representations of Native Americans, European Americans began identifying with Natives on a large scale, as literary critiquing devices, as white Indians, and as mascots. Although images of savage Indian others still found their place in twentieth-century American culture, Native peoples also figured as an integral part of white America's identity (Huhndorf 2001:35). Commandeering the role and the voice of the Native American is an act of (neo)colonial power in which those who have enjoyed the contours of White privilege are able to construct a particular relationship with those who have suffered, historically and into the present, from various forms of White, male hegemony (Springwood 2004:67).

The wide application of white as symbol, in non-racially specific contexts, makes it appear neutral: white as "good" is a Westernized universal abstraction, it just happens that it coincides with people whose skin is deemed white. As Richard Dyer notes, "What is absent from white is any *thing*; in other words, material reality. Cleanliness is the absence of dirt, spirituality the absence of flesh, virtue the absence of sin, chastity the absence of sex and so on" (1997:75). Whiteness is the sum of these social processes which empower those who identify or are viewed as being ethnically white. In the Western world, "whiteness is…a social fact, an identity created and continued with all-to-real consequences for the distribution of wealth, prestige, and opportunity" (Lipsitz 1998:vii). The forms and the powers embedded in whiteness create a social hegemony in which whiteness presides over difference, particularly skin color difference.

The white male fans of FSU sports see themselves vis-à-vis the football team as connected to the romantic notions embedded in the mascot: noble, brave, strong, determined, and courageous. The qualities of whiteness associated with the characteristics viewed within the mascot portrayal serves to heighten the association with the imagined ideal of Indian-ness as it provides for an insular distance of still remaining white while donning Indian qualities as a costume. Particularly at an institutional level such as colleges and universities represent, becoming a graduate of the schools such as FSU makes one a Seminole for life, regardless of racial heritage or background. This is marketing and a consuming of culture via tribalism and ethnicity by hegemonic interests.

Whiteness is set in value in contrast to the Indian, particularly as it is represented by mascots, whiteness is valued above mascots, which themselves are valued over Native Americans. Mascots then represent a middle ground between whiteness and Native Americans, mascots represent the constructed Indian as the go-between of myth and reality. Its value is determined by the historical investment of whiteness in Redness. This separation of reality from culture leads to a vacuum in which Native Americans become lost to a generic popular notion of Indian-ness which becomes back-filled by an American nationalism as a substitute. "As a product of enterprise and imperialism, whiteness is of course always already predicated on racial difference, interaction and domination" (Dyer 1997:13). The ethnocized Other, the non-white peoples within the bounds of the continental United States were considered deficient in some way and were then situated "somewhere between Northern and Western European full 'whiteness' and the clear 'disabilities' suffered by Asian Americans, African Americans, Mexicans, Puerto Ricans, and Native Americans" (Roediger 2008:159).

Whiteness was an ideal that could never be attained by any Other, not only because the valued white skin can never be hue white, but because white as a color is an absence of color, a blank in terms of other colors. In order to be really, absolutely white, or blank in this case, is to be nothing. FSU whiteness appropriates Indian-ness through cultural artifacts and ethnic notions of Seminoles. The idea of "primitive peoples" is an invention of the West which assumes that non-Western (usually nonwhite) cultures are under-civilized. This conception is based on a form of temporal dislocation, wherein the white Westerners exist in "the present and non-whites are living in a more savage, natural, and authentic past-a past which the West has left behind" (Newitz 1997:134). The ideas of the prejudices and barriers of race is a constant influence, one that is never not a factor and never not in play in considering the place of the Other. It is the perceived unconquered spirit of the Seminoles which is desired by non-Native FSU fans who seek to become

Indians through association. The "Other" people are raced, [white people] are just [humans]/people. At the level of racial representation, in other words, whites are not of a certain characteristic race, they are just the "human" race. As such, then, white people view themselves as being able to speak for the human race and because perception is done by whites, people of color can only speak for "their" people. This process of cultural appropriation is a commodification of economic and political power forms.

This contestation is one over the body of the Native American. The body is a discursive site for the grounding of the ideology of whiteness. The difference of skin color is based in this social construct. Colonial imperialists used the body and its coverings as an evaluative tool. The indigenous body represented exotic and erotic modes of display. One of these sites of contention was the World's Fairs phenomena which celebrated the advancements of Western culture on a global scale. White supremacy is the result of practices which allow for the expression of power through white skin color and ethnicity. In one form of expression, it is the ability to mimic subordinate groups in terms of power relationships, often cast as colonized peoples. In terms of mascot presentations it has a long legacy of imitation.

White supremacy is the result of practices which allow for the expression of power through white skin color and ethnicity. In one form of expression, it is the ability to mimic subordinate groups in terms of power relationships, often cast as colonized peoples. In terms of mascot presentations it has a long legacy of imitation. White crowds repeatedly colored themselves via body-painting, and this action is often viewed as a part of popular culture "festivity." From colonial times, there was also a substantial tradition of blackening the skin or of dressing up as Indians "on occasions of festivity, rebellion, and 'misrule.'" It also usually conveyed a "conscious declaration of whiteness and white supremacy" where "Indian impersonation . . . participants 'became' Indians" (Roediger 1999:104). Through white supremacy, whites have become invisible to some degree. Whiteness has enabled "white Americans to stand as unmarked, normative bodies and social selves, the standard against which all others are judged (and found wanting)." The invisibility of whiteness is an "enabling condition for both white supremacy/privilege and race-based prejudice" (Newitz and Wray 1997:3). Thus, the body becomes a discursive site for the colonialized legacy of white supremacy as being viewed as a natural process of the power of whiteness.

White supremacy has been allowed to develop through unequal forms of power. Here, then, "whiteness" had emerged as a relevant category in American life and culture resulting from historic events and conditions such as slavery and segregation, Native American policy and immigration restrictions, conquest and colonialism. Both economics and politics relegated various racial groups to unequal access to property and citizenship, while cultural practices "institutionalized racism in everyday life by uniting diverse European American subjects into an imagined community called into being through appeals to white supremacy . . . helped produce a unified white racial identity through the shared experience of spectatorship" (Lipsitz 1998:3). The superior position of whiteness, thus leading to an idea of white supremacy, a position or location *above* the Other, could be regarded as a natural reaction to viewing inferior others where they are seen to occupy a subordinate location. This whiteness bolstered by exclusiveness, ideology, and economic upward regard can lead to the diminution of the lesser regarded Others. From the white supremacist perspective this is a natural occurrence.

Ethnicity is a cultural construct, one which has sinister structural causes and consequences. Such conscious and deliberate actions have institutionalized group identity in America, through the dissemination of cultural stories and through systematic efforts from colonial times to the present to create economic advantages through a possessive investment in whiteness for European-American colonial settlers. Lipsitz intentionally used each word in this phrase for a reason. They can be parsed as follows. Possessive "is used to stress the relationship between whiteness and asset accumulation in our society" (1998:vii). White supremacy is a system for protecting the privileges of whites by denying the Other opportunities for asset accumulation and upward mobility in American society. Investment highlights how social and cultural forces encourage "white people to expend time and energy on the creation and re-creation of whiteness" and how policies they endorse are consistently shaped by considerations involving race (1998:vii, viii). Through this perspective, white Americans are encouraged to invest in personal whiteness, and to remain true to an identity that provides them with resources, power, and opportunity.

It is by this idea that the creation of the Seminole persona of Osceola becomes grounded. FSU supporters become invested in such a construction of Indian-ness that had been created through such notions of the Noble Savage like stoicism, bravery, spirit, and never surrendering. It is this last criterion that looms large in the rubric of Seminole-ness that had been utilized by the FSU institution. Black has observed that as a graduate of FSU, that "much like that Native who works hard, overcomes challenges, and embraces virtue—so, too, will the university's graduates exhibit these qualities in the workforce and carry them into society to make the world a better place" (2002:614). He also notes the FSU touts this theme when "honoring" the Seminoles by referring to the issue that the tribe had never surrendered to the United States in any of the wars between the two in the nineteenth century. Thus, the FSU graduate emulates this quality of the Seminoles in their own lives, earning this recommendation by being a graduate of the university.

The role of Indian Others in the story of how personal whiteness came to be forces us to see the powerful and lasting ways in which white supremacy transformed settlers' identities by attaching itself to freedom and to ideas concerning gender. This logic of dispossession told of the changes in how "whites thought of themselves, their households, and of their lands, as well as how they thought of those removed from the land" (Roediger 2008:12). White settlers institutionalized a possessive investment in whiteness by pitting people of color against one another. Earlier Europeans did of course note differences between their skin colors and those of non-Europeans, but the idea of "personal whiteness" was something that could be owned as an asset and as an element of identity as it was surely a construct of modernity. David Roediger writes, "The logic of 'whiteness as property,' what Du Bois called 'personal whiteness,' emerged out of the turn to slave modes of production and out of the dispossession of the Indians" (Roediger 2008:27). Further, he observes that "personal whiteness would have to await the slave trade and the settler-colonial conquest of indigenous peoples of the Americas. The notion that one could own a skin color-what the legal scholar Cheryl Harris calls 'whiteness as property' and the historian George Lipsitz calls the possessive investment of whiteness-came into being alongside the reality that only peoples who were, increasingly, being stigmatized by their color could be owned and sold as slaves. It matured alongside the equally brutal notion that land on which the suddenly 'nonwhite' peoples lived would be better managed by 'white' people" (Roediger 2008:1, 2).

The context of modernity as grounded in mascot construction is a mixture of possession, commodification, ownership, and as a meta-form of quasi-slavery in that the Indian persona sought out by mascot institutions can become owned and controlled by the consumer of these processes. The idea of the Indian becomes personalized through the buying of the idealized Indian and the making it into a personalized fetish of white Indian-ness. The Seminole leader Osceola's likeness can be printed upon a T-shirt, sold to fans, and the putting on and wearing of the commodity makes the consumer a Seminole by marketed association and ownership of it. This mechanism connects the past of conquering the Native American body and the present capitalistic form of commodification of the body, manipulating it like a doll such as a jointed body figure like a G.I. Joe who can be bent and twisted to the desire of its possessor. This action reflects the historic fate of the real Osceola whose body had become a public display of conquest by decapitating him and his head becoming a scientific novelty of public display. This reinforces the hegemony of whites adopting and adapting Indian-ness.

In remembering the events which build into the preferred version of the story of American nation-building, the belief in morality and just causes and actions become mythic in their retelling. The processes of imperialism express, in representation, white identities. When a text is one of celebration, it is the manly white qualities of expansiveness, enterprise, courage, and control (of self and others) that are in the foreground. The white male spirit achieves and maintains empire (Dyer 1997:184). In order to provide a foil to this ideological stance of nation-building, there must be an enemy in which to unify the interests of the nation's citizens. The creation of the idea of the "Indian" served this purpose.

Constructing the "savage" other served as an example of what the wilderness held for the fate of the colonialists if they failed in their task of nation-building as a whole. This Other was aimed at building a coherent national consciousness in terms of an "us-versus-them" context of choosing sides, making it a "good-versus-evil" proposition for white Americans. This made it possible to view the dispossession of the Native Americans of their power and possessions legitimate. Because real Indians were understood to be destined to disappear, European Americans considered themselves to be the proper heirs of "Indian-ness" as well as of the land and resources of the conquered Natives. "White America 'owned' Native America; it appropriated Native America for its national past . . . this myth of America gone native at once made the nation unique and shielded it from criticisms of its violent history" (Huhndorf 2001:34, 35). This conflict of cultures meant the replacement or extermination of the constructed idealized Indian.

The practice of white people constructing their own cultural or individual identities in terms of appropriated and misappropriated Native American symbols and traditions began with the very first contact between Europeans and American Indian people. This process claims the right to assess propriety, acceptability, and authenticity in White terms—it is White-centered, White-identified, and White-dominated in these contexts. Thus, defenders of mascots can, "in good faith and with complete sincerity, assert that indigenous symbols and material culture (the feather, for instance) are 'their' traditions that honor native people, precisely because dominant frameworks for adjudicating truth (claims) have been Eurocentric, almost invariably dismissing the validity of indigenous philosophies and perspectives" (King 2004:5, 6). Sustained by ideals of race privilege, those white Americans who support the use of these images and beliefs about American Indians, selectively choose to honor faux American Indians while ignoring the real situations of Native Americans, often "expressing a feigned desire to be a 'redskin' when to live the reality of being labeled a 'redskin' would be intolerable" (Staurowsky 2004:17). A Colonial tradition emerged and continues to thrive in which White institutions locate a person whose Indian-ness is otherwise contested, marginal, or even fabricated to ratify asymmetrical treaties or to counter "undesirable" Native testimony. Such actions serve to freeze Native American people, flattening their cultures and simplifying their histories into stereotypical representations. These stereotypes thus, have interfered with the ability of non-Indian people to see American Indian people as genuinely complex, opinionated, and politically vibrant. In regard to the connections to the overall Indian mascot debates, one must consider the overlapping

American dimensions of colonialism, Whiteness, racial privilege, and oppression. Mascots, then, are a form of playing Indian in which there is an interlocking of economic and emotional investments in the presentation of Indian-ness. It has, therefore, shown itself to be especially persistent and impervious to critique. Indian mascots are, of course, implicated with a much broader tradition of playing Indian, and this practice has sustained itself since at least the time of the Boston Tea Party because of the fantasies and pleasures it has allowed White people to experience (Springwood 2004:68).

In "playing Indian," athletes, sports franchises, and fans allocate Native Americans to a unique and allegorical form of cultural citizenship (Strong 2004:80). Because members of the dominant culture identify with the invented tradition of Indian-ness embodied in mascots, they believe that their intention to honor the Indian warrior tradition, either as the Noble or Ignoble Savage, carries more weight than the dishonor and disrespect experienced by many Native Americans in their own realities and daily lives. Mascot performances such as that of Chief Illiniwek ritually inscribe the relations of colonial and imperial power directly onto the American Indian body, typically represented by a White male student, dressed and painted as the idealized Indian. "It is, in fact, a White male student, like so many patriots and citizens before him, playing Indian, fashioning a self through an enactment of (his understanding of) the indigenous other" (King 2004:3). Dancing mascots thus are the centerpiece in an entertainment vehicle designed to appeal to a White-majority audience that produces a substantial generation of revenue for a primarily all-White leadership structure. It is in institutional spaces as in school settings, where White children and their parents regularly defend their "right" to "Indian" identities and use mascots to their own preferences of Indian display (Staurowsky 2004:13).

Pewewardy has noted that the use of mascots, particularly on the sidelines has a "clown-like" quality to it. However, the quality he speaks of is not one of a comic role, but rather a fool or jester, one that is ridiculed rather than a critiquing element that is a part of some Native American societies (2004:182). There is a meanness that can be more easily connected and attached to this fool/jester role that I see. This attitude can then be more easily transferred toward Native Americans through mascot portrayals. Mascots, thus, are vehicles that carry the cultural baggage of racism and the self-guilt of the Euro-American that becomes directed at an Other of colonialism and its legacy.

Chapter Four

Constructing the Native Voice

When the young Seneca high school student was finishing his first tour around the school gymnasium ending the lap where he began it by the girl's locker room doors, other Seneca youth began to stand in the bleachers and shout out to the young man in cultural drag. Cupping their hands about their mouths they tried to direct their comments to the mascot performer. Although I could not hear what they were saying from my seat in the bleachers across the gym floor, their body language revealed that they were agitated. The Seneca students in the bleachers were trying to communicate their views to the student in Indian costume. They could not be heard above the din created by the non-Native student body cheering on the display of Indianness. These Seneca students were silenced by the majority voice that was enjoying the performance of the Indian mascot. The performer, however, must have heard their comments for, as mentioned before, as he passed by my section of bleachers on his second trip around the gym floor there was confusion in his countenance. As he came by for his third and final lap, his face was more grim in appearance than his appearing amused as he had before when he passed by me for the last time. When the student slipped behind the locker doors, out of sight of the audience, the pageant of Indianness had been finished for that day at least in this school, and the constructed Indian put back into the closet until the next time.

It is also telling that the display of Indian-ness was not an isolated event. Many more episodes have occurred at this location. One such example happened several years later as the football team was in the state playoffs, one young man was dancing on the sidelines during these games, dressed in "fancy-dance" attire. Today, there is a summer pow-wow that takes place on the same football field where the high school competes. In this display of cultural exhibition, the Native people have reappropriated these grounds for their own ends. Competing in a different format of strength and agility, dancers vie against each other for points, rank position, and prize money. In this instance, the Native voice is speaking for itself and is being heard in conjunction with those being entertained by the performances. It is important to point out that the dancers in these competitions are performing pan-tribal dances. This pan-tribal context shows the interconnections between Native American peoples who come together for these events as a form of bridge-building as dance is a traditional form of personal expression and cross-communication.

As another form of pan-tribal context, mascot issues as well have been a form of interconnection made among Native Americans across Native America. This issue is in one sense a gateway issue in that it leads into larger discussions of what is going on in Indian Country. As a popular culture context with which the mainstream has about Native Americans, it can build upon and bring out extent discussions of larger scope and depth.

Many people have commented upon the issues surrounding the mascot debate. Scholars, educators, laity, tribal representatives, and non-Native Americans have input about the contentions of the matter. These perspectives come from psychologists, sociologists, activists, lawyers, school principals, traditional and elected tribal leaders, teachers, and parents. These people will be heard in the constructing of the responses of the Native voice, but the responses will predominantly concentrate on three key consultants that are reflective of the debate and will form the base of the combined Native voice from the local, regional, and national voices commenting on the discourse.[1]

In making a singular voice from the multiple levels of responses, contentions, and perspectives on the matter of Native American-based mascots, the delineating of local, regional, and national viewpoints from key consultants is an aim of this research. The ideas for retaining mascots are the result of forms of power over the Other, which had led to the use of mascots as a hegemonic device geared to present all Native Americans as the idealized Indian Other. The responses to these contentions will combine the responses to these constructed notions of the Indian Other, taken from the Native American people involved with the matter at these multiple levels of interaction. To accomplish this goal, the different contentions which have been generated at these varying levels of discourse seek to counter the reasons as to why mascots should be retained.

The Native American responses presented herein address the contexts of the issues which surround the perceived justification for using and perpetuating ethnocized mascots of American Indians based on their cultures and social modes. The rhetoric is couched in phrases and terminology such as honoring, respecting, and nobility which is then attached to the Native American-as-Indian mascot portrayal. This element of romanticizing the idealized Indian is accomplished through abstract, qualitative words like true, faithful, tradition, and bravery. The rhetoric also includes references to physically quantifiable contexts such as strength, speed, stamina, and endurance. The references point to a physically fit ideal of the Indian as having the characteristics considered laudable by the white masculine audience.

For example, in commenting on the investment of the University of Illinois mascot persona, Chief Illiniwek, in the documentary film, *In Whose Honor?* (1997), Charlene Teters critiques the Indian-as-mascot when she stated, "Of course you love him. You created him." From the same film, Durango Mendoza asks, "What part of 'Ouch!' don't you understand?" when he observes how people at the University of Illinois disregard Native American objections to the mascot portrayal. Also, Arlene B. Hirschfelder (1982) collected material which pointed to the fact that many non-Native American preschool aged children already have formed an idea, usually negative, about Native Americans by the time they start grade school. They arrive at school believing that Indians are inherently violent and that they have feathers growing out of their heads!

A LOCAL PERSPECTIVE

The Salamanca school district regards itself as unique in the New York State public school system and rightly so (Ward letter 2001). First, the public school district resides on land located within the boundaries of a Native American reservation. The Seneca Nation of Indians is the landowner of the site upon which the tenant City of Salamanca resides. Salamanca city officials make a claim of this notoriety by stating that, "Salamanca is the only city in the world that is located on an Indian reservation" (SNI 2002). This claim is diluted as Palm Springs, California, and Espanola, New Mexico, also both are located on respective reservation lands. A second noteworthy feature about the Salamanca School District is that the student body is made up of 26 percent Native students (Ward interview 2001). This is one of the highest concentrations of Native American students enrolled in a NYSED public highs school district. There are thirteen "contracting for Indian education school districts" in the state. Only two other districts have such an equitable population of Native students. A third characteristic is that of the imagery that is associated with the Warrior name. The modern Warrior logo is specific and culturally appropriate for the Seneca community (White 2001). Prior to 1978, SHS used a stereotypic representation of a long, feathered "war bonnet"-styled headdress and profile of a Lakota/Plains type of Native American to depict their Warrior.

In 2001, the Salamanca High School student body, through a poll taken by district superintendent, voted to keep its name and logo with 94 percent of the students who voted in favor of retaining the name "Warriors" (Ward interview 2001). The students had been presented with other options like Wildcats, Engineers, and Wolfpack and voted on those given choices (Ward interview 2001). Superintendent Mark J. Ward then brought the matter to the attention of former Seneca Nation of Indians Higher Education Program (SNIHEP) Coordinator Donald White, who then went before the SNI tribal council with this information. The tribal council voted nearly unanimously to support the stance taken by the students, directing him to write a supporting letter to be sent along with Superintendent Ward's response (Huff 2001). The city school board, under the leadership of its president, Ann O'Brien, voted unanimously to support the student's position (O'Brien interview 2002). This led to the City of Salamanca Common Council taking up the action and voting to support the students and the school district. This is something of note to get all parties concerned to be overwhelmingly supportive of one another on an issue, particularly in the matter of this issue (Yonker 2001). In response to the NYSED Commissioner Mills' letter, Superintendent Mark J. Ward put together a packet of information, which he then sent back to Mills' office, containing a profile of the student body and the poll results, the resolutions from the school board, the SNI tribal council, and the Salamanca city council supporting the high school (Vecchiarella 2001), hoping to prove to Mills that all sides in this community desire to keep Salamanca High School the "Home of the Warriors."

The Seneca people of the Allegany Indian Reservation have been in contention with the SHS school district over mascots and logos since the early 1970s (Bilharz 1998:104). The rise of Native American civil rights movement on a national scale, called Red Power, during the 1960s through the 1970s demonstrated to Native Americans that they could affect changes in the way the non-Native public see this group of people. Native American groups comprising the Red Power movement gained visibility through media exposure of their actions at the national level. These protests served as examples for the localized contentious actions used by the smaller communities of Native people, much the same way the lunch counter sit-ins and bus boycotts became associated with the African American civil rights movement. Beginning with the "fish-ins" supporting treaty rights of tribes in the Pacific Northwest in the early 1960s, occupations of sites and property takeovers became the Native American "way" of protesting (Josephy, Nagel, and Johnson 1999:1). These protests had many influencing factors such as education, cultural appropriation, economic, and political criteria (Josephy, Nagel, and Johnson 1999:93). The 1970s were full of such actions as walk-outs and other protests that were copied by Senecas at Salamanca, which showed the discontent of the Seneca students at the attitudes of the school and its staff people when dealing with Native Americans at SHS.

One person that has seen the contentions of the SHS mascot is Sue John. As a home-school-liaison for the school district she works directly with the

Seneca students and their issues in this district. She has much first-hand experience with the debate.

> Yes, when I was in high school we had a situation one year that the cheerleaders wanted to have a mascot. At that time the mascot symbol used was not of an Iroquois. Rather, it was a profile of an Indian in a full headdress. It was nothing that represented us here. The mascot was a cheerleader who somehow purchased a traditional outfit from an Indian woman and attempted to wear it at a pep assembly. She came running out in that outfit or maybe it was the football players that carried her out like an Indian princess. They set her down and she began to prance around and the Indian girls, oh man, we got all angry and upset with that. We couldn't all believe it was happening. We immediately took steps to protest that. We thought that was wrong, it didn't belong out there. It was an insult in almost every way you could think of. We did take action and staged a walk-out, sit-down type of protest. (Sue John interview 2000)

Some walk-outs lasted several days. Others were timed to coincide on a Friday afternoon, possibly to get out of school early that week.

As a home-school liaison between the Seneca Nation of Indians and the SHS system, Sue John's personal experiences tell of the local and national influences that the movement had upon her and the choices she made along the way, coming back to Salamanca High School (John interview 2000). One example of the lack of sensitivity that she and her peers had to deal with was at a "pep" assembly for the football team where a white cheerleader had come into possession of a traditional Seneca woman's outfit and wore it at this assembly of high school students who were supposedly honoring the winning tradition of Warrior football. The older Seneca girls in the audience were outraged, some to the point of crying frustrated tears at such a disrespectful display by the school. Sue and another student organized a walk-out that operated in shifts so that students joining in the protest could do so during a free period and not miss any classes in the school day. Sue and the other girl were the ones who decided that they would face the brunt of the punishment for this action. The two of them were inspired by protests that had taken place across Native America. The idea of a walk-out styled protest had been modified from those that they had seen and learned from the AIM actions that Sue had seen on the television (John interview 2000). This action brought in the parents of some of the students in support of their concerns to meet with school administrators and begin a dialogue.

Sue John tells of the display of privilege and power as demonstrated through the tacit approval of "playing Indian" by the SHS district.

> Yes, when I was in high school we had a situation one year that there was a cheerleader who somehow purchased a traditional outfit from an Indian woman and she began to prance around and the Indian girls, oh man, we got all

angry and upset with that. We couldn't all believe it was happening. We immediately took steps to protest that. We thought that was wrong, it didn't belong out there. It was an insult in almost every way you could think of. We did take action and staged a walk-out, sit-down type of protest. The Seventies were famous for their protests. We knew where to draw the line and not get in to too much trouble. We took people out of their study halls to protest. The main organizers stayed there all day and got in the most trouble. We got publicity on that and attention. Then, we got the parents to come up and join us and support us. That stopped it for a while. That was one that I thought was real offensive and the community did respond to that...We were more up on Indian life at that time. We were very aware at that time when we were kids. We looked at issues on a national level. I don't know where that came from except maybe that the American Indian Movement was very strong at that time and we were looking at some of the protests going on across the country in Wounded Knee, Alcatraz, those types of movements. The BIA take-over was in our minds. We realized that we do have rights and we have to speak up for them. If that hadn't have happened, on a national level, that kind of movement, we may not have felt strong enough or empowered enough to do it, to stand up as kids, to stand up for our rights. (John interview 2001)

On the day she graduated from high school, she made a vow "never to return" as she looked in her rearview mirror and left Salamanca. These days, she works for the district and her office is now located in the room once occupied by the principal before whom she once had to sit and attempt to bring these issues into the open. When asked why she returned to this school, she replied that she "did it for the kids" (John interview 2001).

The frustration of past experiences has led Seneca people such as John back to the school district in order to aid Seneca youth educational interests in any possible fashion. As she explains below, she believes her presence is needed because the Native American students must have someone from their own community with whom they can discuss problems when the need arises.

I remember being on a committee with the [Seneca] Nation officials and different ones and we went in and started doing 'talking circles', talking with the kids documenting grievances, issues, interviewing, getting documentation of physical abuse and abuse we could not see happening. Overt, overt and covert, I guess. So, when I heard the kids talking, of how many of our kids had the same story, that there was no one in that school for them, and it was true. They didn't have no one to talk to. There was no Indians there that could witness the abuse. If something happened, if someone got slammed up against the radiator by a teacher, they had no place to run, they couldn't tell no one. Who was going to believe them? There's no Indians about for them to go to. So, the first thing I did, and it really hit me hard that I did, was that I ran for the school board. (John interview 2000)

Not every member of the Seneca Nation is as sensitive about the Salamanca Warrior as Sue John. In fact, some parents feel that the mascot issue has no relevance to the make-up of their children and that they were not affected by participating in sports represented by the tribally inappropriate mascot. For example, Robin Crouse, mother of a Warrior athlete notes:

> I am trying to think, like, with Billy, he was playing because he was on the team. You know what I mean? It wasn't like he felt like he was a big bad fighter warrior. He didn't portray that image. It was, you know, he was a part of the team, a part of the, you know what I mean. To me that is how my son acted. It was never like, you know, like he was like, you know, going in there to be some big bad, bad-ass Indian, you know what I mean. It wasn't like that with him. (Crouse interview 2004)

The variable responses from parents and school staff reflect the ambiguous responses of opinion of Native people on the matter. The following different perspectives view the contention at two levels: one seeing a larger picture of the issue where a context of social justice is recognized, and of a second viewpoint, one that seeks to recognize the cultural investment of the community with a culturally resonant symbol of their heritage.

Sue John remarks on the former and current SHS mascot logo and its multiple levels of meanings for Native American observers in the Seneca and Salamanca communities.

> Some are sensitive about it. There are a few people like myself that find it offensive. So, it's kind of a mixed reaction. I haven't chosen as yet to write to the Salamanca Press or to the district or anything like that. I wouldn't want to get people angry or anything like that; stirred up about it. Although I may do it in the future, you never know. My preference is that we don't use Indian people as mascots. My definition of a mascot is an untrue or false person, or a sub-human being like a bulldog or something like leprechauns. I've always felt that a mascot wasn't ever anything that was taken serious or a real human being and I don't think Indians should be viewed that way. The "Warriors" isn't like that Cleveland Indians mascot, that big Indian guy. Their logo, looking like a cartoon Indian is not quite at that degree. We could look at other names fitting for our sports logo. (John interview 2001)

What is she is speaking about is the current Warrior logo. It is of a traditional Seneca sachem wearing a signifier of a man's leadership or public office: a *gus:tow:weh*. This headdress is reserved for traditional government male leadership. It has a tight-fitting crown of small feathers. What signifies its wearer as a Seneca leader is the single large feather atop the cap. The Senecas have one such feather to denote their leadership in chief's council meetings. Other member nations of the Haudenosaunee have differing combinations of one to three feathers in varying positions to denote which nation the men belong and represent in council. This left-facing profile of a Seneca leader was drawn by Seneca artist Carson R. Waterman.

Cheryl Signore also works in the school district serving in a co-capacity as an aide to Sue John. Cheryl Signore was a student and a parent of her children attending Salamanca High School.

> Because of that, our unique situation being on the reservation here, that we would be allowed to keep that as our mascot. That the students didn't find it offensive—the Native American student body didn't find it offensive. And in light of that, we would request that we keep that as our mascot. (Signore interview 2004)

By working directly with the Seneca students at SHS, Signore has a view that incorporates what the students discuss outside of the hallways. She works in the Indian Education Office for the district. Her interaction with the students is something with which she is concerned for as she serves as an advocate for their issues. She feels that the Seneca students find the contemporary logo something of cultural significance which they can share and find a source of pride about. The administration apparently did not garner the full significance of this message because a few years later a Seneca youth was dressed up in Lakota/Plains regalia for one of these pep assemblies in the high school gym, taking a few laps around the court, raising a tomahawk a few times as he went 'round the floor. After the assembly other Seneca students were asking why the student did such a thing. He did it only once, for he received enough chiding and teasing that he never did that again.

> No, they haven't done anything like that, you know, even when my son was playing basketball or football or lacrosse. They, you know, when he was in school they didn't. There was nothing like that. But, it seems like I remember that picture of Ike being in one of the yearbooks now that you say that. That wouldn't be too cool. I don't know who set him up to do that. (Crouse interview 2004)

Seneca youth in varying perspectives as well had taken proactive actions to establish their positions along the points of the localized issues surrounding the matter.

Tribal concerns became translated into support for the children and the position taken by the tribal entity lends legitimacy to the rendered work by Seneca artist, Carson R. Waterman.

> No, it went over quite easily. We just presented it to the Council and again half of the Council is made up of people from Allegany, or the Salamanca students and they expressed the same thing. It sort of echoed all those things we have talked about. You know the athletes saying no in finding warrior offensive. And again everybody says, "Hey, that is a Seneca Person drawn by a Seneca Artist." That whole routine, you know. They said the same thing "Leave it

alone, leave it alone." We didn't have to convince nobody. (White interview 2002)

One consultant found that there was support for the mascot logo because of the cultural distinction the symbols represent to the Seneca community. Robin Crouse was a student at the school and has sent three children through the district. Her children were involved in athletic as well as cultural activities in the school.

> I think for Title IX it was brought up, I was on the parent committee, I still am. You know, as what we felt as parents and the same things is that we didn't feel that it needed to be changed, you know what I mean. That some places [needed to change their mascot portrayals,] yes. But we felt here in our own community because you know it is almost like you take pride in it. "It" being a Salamanca Warrior. So but I know that the parents that were on the Parent Committee at that time everybody thought that we didn't need to, you know, we didn't even want to address it with the, you know, we didn't want to go and raise a big stink with the school about it. You know, they wanted it so. (Crouse interview 2004)

Another consultant, herself a Salamanca graduate as well, has seen both sides of the debate from her fifteen years' experience in working for the district in the Indian Education Office. Cheryl Signore's position is that she would help out the students with whatever decision that they made on the issue at various times over her tenure at the Salamanca district. She feels that the district would not exist without the students so she works to support them.

> To myself as to why would we get rid of the mascot that says who we are. It is a representation of who we are. And I think to some extent the kids enjoy the other students from other districts sort of being scared of them not only because of the mascot because they were Native, they were Indian children. And there was a little bit of they were supposed to be *fierce* I guess or something to be feared. And they kind of enjoyed that to a point. (Signore interview 2004)

Donald White offers another view, especially of his high school days. White lives on another of the Seneca Nation of Indians reservations in New York, the Cattaraugus Indian Reservation, and tells of himself and his fellow students at another high school, Gowanda High School, and how some viewed the position of the Seneca students that attended Salamanca.[2] He stated that there was very little in the way of Native support at his high school during the 1960s and that the Native presence through the name and image of Warriors at Salamanca seemed enviable to him and others. "We were Panthers. What can you do with a Panther for Native pride?" White asks. He pointed out the unique situation of Salamanca schools and of their location on a reservation; when Commissioner Mills's letter came out, he approached the SNI tribal council to sponsor a resolution to support the high school and its wish to retain the Warrior name and imagery (White interview 2002). "It's appropriate," White says of the school keeping the Warrior at Salamanca. "It's culturally sensitive and it's accepted," he said, referring to the Warrior mascot (Champagne 2001:1). Adds Adrian John, the imagery "fits the community" (A. John interview 2002). Maxine Dowler, the only Seneca on the city school board and a former teacher in the district, said "she hasn't heard anything negative about keeping the Warrior mascot" (Champagne 2001:1).

The meaning for the Seneca community was one viewpoint that was used to get tribal support for the school's position.

> We would rather take a position of fixing any incorrect image. I don't know, working with the school district to make it work. And to make it, I guess, culturally sensitive and culturally specific. Because again, as Native People, as Indians, um, I know I went to Gowanda and that was way back in the 60's and we wanted something Indian in that school and I don't know if that would have come out to be culturally sensitive or anything like that. But because we know that, you know, around here is basically about 27% of the kids that are Native. And it is the same thing down in Gowanda but as a former student in Gowanda it is just like, "Man, there are a lot of Indians here, man, we ought to have something Native, something Indian," and we didn't. And we used to actually look here at Salamanca going, "Man, that is pretty cool they are called the Warriors, you know." (White interview 2001)

SNIHEP Coordinator Todd Waite offers a perspective that reflects White's observations. Waite did encounter a sideline Native American mascot in college, and along with others there, did seek out the means to change the spectacle.

> It is a difficult situation, especially on a reservation, because growing up in Salamanca, you know, the Warrior was always, you know, the mascot and point of pride for the school and you grow up kind of accepting it. Because it is the nature of the school and the community. As I look back on Salamanca they really tried to be respectful of the mascot from a high school level here. It wasn't a real caricature, it wasn't a comedic sort of thing. (Waite interview 2004)

While the public school district may feel that the presence of Native people in its population is cited as an example of multiculturalism, the image used by the district and revered by the SNI, it is one that is a former reminder of what the Allegany Senecas had once been.[3]

> Well, since I've been working at Salamanca as a guidance counselor that question has been brought up twice by the administration. It seems to be cyclical. The first time was five years ago when I first arrived. The superintendent first approached me saying, "Gee, wouldn't it be nice if we had an Indian

mascot being the 'Warriors'? It's a sensitive area. I know in the past the community had an uprising against that. Maybe you could check that out." He said that to all of the Indian Education staff in a meeting. None of us took any action from that to let it drop and nothing came from it. Probably early last year the high school principal brought the question up again in his office that we could possibly talk to the Indian community if the time is right for us to have some kind of a mascot. He promised that it could be done very culturally sensitive. It could be a Native American, and to have something done during the pep assemblies, and possibly at the Homecoming during the halftime activities. He suggested maybe some of the Indian dances from whoever wants to participate. I didn't answer him at the time. I was surprised that he would even bring that subject up again. I didn't have an answer right then. (John interview 2001)

Much of the debate centers on the meaning of the word "warrior" in the context of the unique confines of Salamanca schools and the city itself often in contrast with each other and also with the Seneca interests. The argument is that "warriors" is a generic term that can be applied to most societies or cultures that have such roles for males/men. Heron feels that this applies to the tradition of some cultural groups, such as the Senecas at Salamanca, that are part of the overall responsibilities of this group's men (Heron interview 2002). Don White applies the meaning of the traditional Seneca definition to refer to the "young men" of the group (White interview:2002). In the discourse over the high school use of this imagery, a "warrior" is "more than a name" ("What's In a Name?," *The Salamanca Press* 2001:1). Further, a Warrior is defined, by Salamanca athletic standards, as having courage to struggle and pass a test. This gives moral and/or mental strength to the image and to have been led by example of older Warriors who pass on their wisdom and inspiration to further tradition via football, for these young men are molded into Warriors as "The Tradition Continues!" ("What's In a Name?," *The Salamanca Press* 2001:1).

> In the community we have a group of boys like eleven or twelve [years old] that have a football team and their team or one of their teams is called the "Redskins." I've seen their name in the paper and I personally am offended. I find that offensive. Before I went and did anything drastic or radical or made a big stink about it I thought about it. I spoke to some of the parents in the community and I get answers. Some are offended but don't feel strongly about it. I would say half of the people that I talk to, that's about twenty families, haven't given it any thought because it doesn't matter one way or the other. (John interview 2001)

In 1992, there was a change in the population of the city of Salamanca. Due to a population decline, the city could only field two youth squads, and the West End and the East End teams had to combine. The West End team was named the Warriors. The East End team was called the Blue Devils. The parents of the two organizations were at odds over a name for the combined team. A conflict arose when in combining the two squads into one, the parents of the East End team did not want their kids to become Warriors just yet. Such is the loyalty to tradition of youth football in this place.

Tyler Heron, youth football coach, also a former tribal councilor, decided to let the kids settle their parents' differences. The kids chose the name of the new team: "Redskins." Heron is of course aware of the meaning of the name "Redskins" and its historical origins as the proof needed for collecting bounty. In other words, the bloody skins, scalps, ears, and other pieces taken from the bodies of Native Americans who were hunted and killed during the eras of expansion in colonial America. The children seem to be unaware of the term's pejorative legacy. As this example shows, the racism that is constructed by the dominant society has been internalized by the children of the community, both Native and non-Native alike, and the use of the term by a Native coached and populated team has no qualm over the name from its players and staff, and from some of the Native American players' parents' point of view, as well. However, there are some parents and other staff people who have a different perspective. They find the name use troublesome. Heron said, "That's what happens when you let kids decide things." He commented further, "The Redskins were the (NFL) champs that year. If the Steelers were champs, then they'd have called themselves the Steelers." With the mascot controversy becoming larger in national scope, the West End Redskins have become Warriors once again (from 1998) in the present (Heron interview 2002).

A REGIONAL PERSPECTIVE

Doug George-Kanentiio arrived on the Syracuse University campus after attending college in New Mexico (George-Kanentiio interview 2002). Leaving his home region for an education elsewhere offered George his first pan-Native experience and the opportunity to learn from Native people that had learned from others from across the country. This knowledge is transitional because George's and his cohorts' deeds were the link in the chain of protest action and identity politics that had such incarnations through the years as the National Indian Education Association, the National Indian Youth Council and the American Indian Movement.

As he explains in the following excerpt, George-Kanentiio's actions eventually led him back to his home territories of the Haudenosaunee Confederacy.

> I was a student of the University of New Mexico in the spring of '77 and decided to come transfer east to a school here. And I thought Syracuse would

be a good place to not only pursue my area of the two majors I was interested, History and Journalism. We could become a magnet if we could get together a bunch of Native Students and begin to work with the administration and begin to offer programs that would enhance peoples understanding of Native People and at the same time would provide an incentive for Native Students to go to Syracuse or to go to university, you know, generally. (George-Kanentiio interview 2002)

After learning of the antics of the then sideline mascot, Doug George-Kanentiio decided to find as many Native American students as possible enrolled at SU, to try to contact them and organize a student group (George-Kanentiio interview 2002). In order to get the necessary "critical mass" of supporters and resources to organize and make claims against SU and its administration, the students had to first find one another among the numbers of enrolled students at Syracuse University (Tarrow 1994:81).

Building a movement from within the academic system and educational bureaucracy by the Native American interests in the debate needed an impetus, a starting energy that coalesced around the protest of the racialized Native American-as-team mascot portrayal. According to consultant interviews about the actions and the era of the movement actions, there had been some concern expressed over the dancing sideline mascot, particularly during the football season of the fall 1977 semester at Syracuse University (Honyoust interview 2002). This was the campus topic that dominated the attention of the institution and surrounding community for that semester (George-Kanentiio interview 2002). George-Kanentiio's ideas on how to approach the SU administration and how to frame the claims of the student group against the mascot made this so.

Initially it was a person that did look Iroquois with the Mohawk style haircut and things, but it actually became one with the war bonnet and that kind of thing. So it was a dishonorable thing in the first place that anybody would desecrate Indian remains and elevate it to a position to where it became, you know, intertwined with the school's self-perception on its image. But that never did happen, they never did find the remains and that was just a myth, and so, and the Chancellor knew this, you know, and he was a nice guy, very patient, soft spoken person and he realized there was a need to divest this school of this silliness. . . . And this one in particular had little to do with the Iroquois visually and if that was the case then it certainly couldn't bring honor to the Iroquois because there was no substance to it. There was no attempt to use the mascot in a way that would enhance people's understanding of the Iroquois. There was nothing to it, it was a shallow one-dimensional type of image. And it was founded on what initially started out to be a joke.[4] (George-Kanentiio interview 2002)

Though the Onkwehonwehneha group served as a focal point of on-campus student protests against the use of the Saltine Warrior mascot, it was one of many actions undertaken by students in this era. According to David C. Smith, who served as an academic advisor for the student group, the actions by Doug George and his cohort were a small contention in relation to other preceding protests against the Viet Nam war. The Native students' activities were one of many contentious voices raised up during a period of social restructuring and active, student-led protests (Smith interview 2005).

The Native American student's group pointed out that the portrayal of the Saltine Warrior is that of the Lakota, not the Onondaga. The warlike, wrathful portrayal was grossly unfair and historically incorrect. Rather this group felt that there should be an emphasis on Native American recruitment, programs, and courses that would provide a realistic picture of Native people from the Syracuse University administration (Onkwehonwenena 1978). These were some of the claims that the student group wanted the administration to follow through on for an improved opportunity for other Native students that would come to the university after this cohort of students finished their tenure at SU. Onkwehonwehneha was not only acting in their interests but also for future interests as these people would become trailblazers for others to follow that sought out a postsecondary education.

> And the actions of this mascot were cartoonish and I thought obscured real appreciation for the Iroquois. And it was just offensive. It looked silly. It was perpetuating harmful stereotypes and no effort was made to try to temporize that by the school by offering the students access to formal going to classes that might have given them a better appreciation as to this area's original heritage. The school didn't offer anything really. And so when I came, transferred to Syracuse, the first thing I did was find out how many other students were attending and I believe we had 35 Native students enrolled at Syracuse at that time. And there wasn't a Native Student organization so I decided, "Well, let's call the students together and see if there is interest in forming one." And in fact there was and we did create a Native Student's Organization. And we wanted to rid the University of the mascot, but we also wanted to use that effort as a way of revising the school that was in need for changes, you know. (George-Kanentiio interview 2002)

The goals of the group not only included the demand to get rid of the Saltine Warrior, but also to see an opportunity to educate the campus, possibly offering courses on Iroquois history and traditions and how the university had appropriated such images and idealizations of Native Americans (George-Kanentiio interview 2002). In this one way, the group hoped to "stimulate people's interest in Native people rather than become a source of contention . . . as a way to take hold of this issue and make it work in a positive way" (George-Kanentiio interview 2002). Through the attention gained from their actions, Onkwehonwehneha wanted to broaden the frame of their claims to include other resources for education and services on campus.[5] This broadening of the focus of their claims also created space for more potential resources for the cause.

> And so I thought, "Well, if we could get these, some programs started. A Native Studies Program, a Native Residence, you know. Native People within the administration." That kind of thing. And it was something that was very badly needed in New York State. And there wasn't any school that offered it. Though I said, "Well, the institution in Syracuse seemed a good place." (George-Kanentiio interview 2002)

> The Saltine Warrior is a "racist symbol," says the SU Native American group who have condemned the mascot as degrading therefore racist. Such issues have to be critically assessed, and such a question becomes emotional and not susceptible to rational discussion. The Saltine Warrior presents an exaggerated caricature that as a symbol imparts characteristics to all American Indians. This representation suggests that Indians are by nature aggressive, violent, uncontrolled, and somewhat boorish. There are those who support the Saltine Warrior and do so out of pride as a tradition, not in malice to Native Americans. But, [done] in pride as a tradition balanced against those aggrieved by such representation where the logical solution is to find a new mascot. (Abernathy 1977)

Anti-Native American sentiment began to surface in the commentary of the debate in the media. Some commentators called the student group "mean-spirited" and that such a minority could be influencing the policy for the majority (Shefflin 1977, Pasho 1978). Other commentators were defending their creation, "our Indian," against the "real" Indians who wanted to end the tradition that went along with football games being played on crisp fall afternoons on "the Hill," the "decision to drop the mascot was really yielding to the demands of a few people by SU [and] he finds it disgusting to do so" (Masters 1978). Other commentary focused on the administration giving into special interests and of not consulting with the larger non-campus community that had no direct ties with the university other than that of a shared geography: "the Saltine Warrior is a victim of our new racial consciousness. Onkwehonweneha has sunk to an astounding depth of meanness and silliness" (Poe 1977). These sentiments from the non-university contingent made up the bulk of the commentary in favor of the mascot and against the Native Americans and their supporters at SU. Much feeling came across from this larger community of not having any input in the decision or of the investment in the SU culture of the city of Syracuse.

> And we felt very good about it, and we anticipated the hostility of the alumni and sure enough it came and drove in waves. You know initially our first year

was people were extremely upset, but it gradually faded, you know, over the next couple years and every once in a while some person would bring it up and especially in the dark days in sports team especially in the football team in the early '80s when they thought, "Oh, we eliminated Saltine Warrior now look what happened to us." (George-Kanentiio interview 2002)

Some contend that:

> [T]he Saltine Warrior is not racist, rather it is the epitome of Indian pride, it represents a legendary figure. Onkwehonweneha, which has only 33 members did the impossible (?!). The group scared the daylights out of the SU administration. It said the magic word, it screamed "Discrimination!" While others call in SU's compliance with civil rights and Title IX money in regard to women's athletics, so the Saltine Warrior is out. Not because it was unpopular but behind a façade of appeasing one injured group lies a predictable story of appeasing the pocketbook. (Stashenko 1978)

The connection between minorities, the threat of litigation, and money is made by this author who feels that such special interests have too much influence. The realization of the context of athletic mascots has more implications as to funding and spending of resources on all athletic programs for men and women as a federal policy.

Others associated with the university in some aspect were heard from as well. Boosters and alumni threatened to stop donating to the university at the loss of the icon that represented their time at SU. Some threatened to have their names removed from the list of supporters of the university, how "would Jim Thorpe react to the Saltine Warrior nonsense? He wants SU to remove his name from the Alumni Roster in protest" (Tucker 1978). Others wrote in to newspapers that other colleges and universities were keeping their Indian mascots, so why could not Syracuse University keep its rendition of the mascot on the sidelines? "SU played the University of Miami, Ohio, Redskins with their American Indian mascot.[6] If the Washington Redskins, the Cleveland Indians, the Miami, Ohio, Redskins, Dartmouth Indians, the Atlanta Braves, C. Michigan Chippewas, the Golden State Warriors can adopt Indian names, why not SU?" (The Syracuse *Post Standard* 1980). After the Saltine Warrior had been retired from public display, boosters tried to have someone dressed in a similar costume in the stands, and tried to get this person onto the sidelines. This person was arrested for trespassing and escorted from the building. Also, the sentiment was carried from generations of SU alumni and students. Several letters to the media informed that their sons had the "honor" of playing Indian for SU, and that this was the highlight of their offspring's days at the university (Masters 1978), and as alumni, their opinions, and monetary support, should count for something in the debate. Current students, many from the SU Greek system of sororities and fraternities also tried to save the mascot. Their interests were in support of the Lambda Chi Alpha fraternity from whose ranks comes the chosen impersonator dressed in Indian headdress and "French-styled fringed clothing" (George-Kanentiio interview 2001).

> Put them in another position, you know, for us would be a source of strength and for them would be something that would be unique. It would be to our advantage actually because we were familiar with the procedures and the Onondaga, in many cases the members of the Council were the parents of some of the students there. And it would give us an advantage and would also serve as an attraction for the fraternity because they would see something they never had access to before which is a functioning Native government. And maybe would give them insight to how Native people think. (George-Kanentiio interview 2002)

A factor that turned out to be a key for the Onkwehonwehneha group was their asking of the Onondaga Chiefs council for advice on the issue. It was this action that had brought an external source as a resource for their assistance that the debate took on a more personal and deeply felt concern over the issue from the Native American camp. Andy Burns, the Lambda Chi Alpha fraternity brother that was the "Last" Saltine Warrior, met with Onondaga members at the reservation to see how they felt about the mascot. Burns criticized the SU Native American group of going against the wishes of the majority. He thought the administration buckled under pressure (Coffey 1978). As the symbol of conflict and of SU, the central character in the debate is the persona of the Saltine Warrior. The real human counterpart of this construct is the fraternity brother that got caught up in the politicized struggle over social justice and cultural significance and the modes of tradition and institutionalized racism that are on opposing sides. He criticized real Native people from a perspective that was veiled by stereotypic ideals of what things Indian were comprised. Because the Native American students and the Onondaga Nation did not act in expected behaviors of compliance and being friendly, Burns cast them as minorities and symbols of a larger force that uses pressure tactics to get their ways.

According to George, there were certain men whose roles as chiefs were influential in the debate process. Several of these men are now passed such as Tadodaho, or Voice of the Confederacy, Leon Shenandoah, and Onondaga Chiefs Irving Powless Sr., and Paul Waterman. Other members of the council included Irving Powless Jr. and Oren Lyons ('58), an alumnus of Syracuse University. These are men remembered by George for their methodical and patient proceedings in listening to both sides of the debate.[7] In October 1977, the various sides met several times at the Onondaga Nation council house, in the same building used by the Haudenosaunee Confederacy when it meets and conducts business collectively. The Lambda Chi Alpha fraternity, when speaking, emphasized tradition in their presentation (Huff interview 2001). The Native students emphasized the retiring of the mascot, but also other services and support from SU. The chiefs listened to both sides, then, began their own deliberations on the matter. After coming to a decision, Shenandoah spoke to the audience to tell them that the chiefs supported the retirement of the mascot and the reasons why the chiefs did so. He then thanked the fraternity brothers. The fraternity brothers seemed impressed by the manner and process in which the deliberations were handled by the chief's council. George remembers most of all how Shenandoah spoke in a quiet and respectful manner (George-Kanentiio online interview 2004).

After the various student organizations met with the chief's council and were exposed to the council's operations and openness for the many perspectives of debate, even the pro-mascot side began to view the issue in the council's light and were moved to realize the impropriety of the mascot and its derivative, stereotypic presentation for public display and consumption. The last white fraternity brother that "played Indian" on the sidelines even went as far as distancing himself from his fraternal organization after having been involved in the discourse with the chief's council (Huff interview 2001). His faux rendition of a "chief" was so far removed from the reality he witnessed for himself that he was humbled and became aware and conscious that the mascot role play must be ended.

The community of the Onondaga Nation had no real economic clout with which to press the Syracuse University administration over the mascot issue. Their leverage or bargaining power in the matter was couched in moralist and cultural frames that sought to show the portrayals fostered and promoted by the university of such a small and cohesive group of people were wrong and that the mascot performance must end. The decision reached by the chief's council was explained to both sides and the council thanked all for their input on the matter (George-Kanentiio online interview 2004).

The approach taken by Onkwehonwehneha sought to be open and appreciative as possible to other viewpoints in the discourse as what had exhibited for them by the chiefs' council.

> We were never hostile towards anybody regardless of how firmly they felt about the Saltine Warrior. We had learned our lesson at Onondaga that is diplomacy, calm reasoning and, you know, the arts of persuasion. And it worked for us. We did not have to confront anybody. We did not have to have any demonstration. Unlike other schools where unfortunately, you know, the Native Students failed to persuade the administration or the Alumni because once you engage in a highly publicized event that people take sides, you know, either for or against. We tried to find a middle ground; we tried to just ask a simple question why not? And here are the reasons and by entering into our world and our reality and being able to deal from a perspective of cultural and historical strength we were able to achieve the removal of that image where

the students, like say the University of Illinois and other schools have not been that successful. You know, and we just brought the Iroquois history [and processes of conflict resolution] and applied it to the current situation and it worked for us. (George-Kanentiio interview 2002)

The Orangemen are without a mascot. The Saltine Warrior no longer reigns victorious. Concerned that the mascot offered a stereotypic portrait of American Indians, the Office of Student Affairs decided to drop the mascot entirely. Mounts said the new mascot should incite support of the crowd for SU Athletics. There have been some humorous suggestions—Saltine Crackers or SUnkist Orange, no buckskinned, befeathered figure will lead the Orangemen. Only the statue will remain, a memento of a rich Syracuse tradition that is no more. (*Alumni News* 1978)

The Saltine Warrior bronze by Kaisch ('46)[8] is now the only Noble Savage-derived Indian that survives on the SU campus from the contested debate over the use of Native Americans as team mascots for entertainment purposes. The evolution of the identity of the SU athletic teams having a flexible constructed identity that has been remade, even in the present: now there are no references to race or gender as now the Orangemen, and Orangewomen, are called the Orange in 2004, as in the color, not necessarily the fruit. The Saltine Warrior enjoyed a run of twenty-four years along the sidelines of SU athletics games before it was ended in 1978 and forty-five years overall in the graphic imagination of the university. And at the end of the spring sports season, the Saltine Warrior danced off into the sunset; Andy Burns, the Lambda Chi Alpha fraternity brother selected to perform the impersonation that season, would be the last of his kind.

A NATIONAL PERSPECTIVE

The connection between the University of Illinois and the nation-wide level of attention by Native American groups and interests, along with their supporters, lies in the protest against the mascot and the initiating of the discourse through its refusal to retire its half-time sideline performer, Chief Illiniwek. In 1975, a national representative of the American Indian Movement, AIM, Clyde Bellecourt, spoke at the UI campus to point out the inaccuracy of the Chief Illiniwek portrayal and the racism in which it is grounded (Teters, *The Illio* 1975:154). In response, the second Chief Illiniwek performer, A. Webber Borchers, then a Republican Party State Representative from Decatur, defended the tradition by saying the dance at halftime is "the most outstanding tradition of any university in the land" with no disrespect intended for the Indians (Teters, *The Illio* 1975:154, 155). This comment by Borcher's is in his semi-recognition of the problematic complaints by Native Americans in his hearing and understanding of the contentions. In a backhanded way he speaks of the bothersome issues of inauthenticity and cultural appropriation of Indian-ness by the UI. He tries to gloss this contention over with an appeasing no disrespect intended, for the comments spoken of by the Native Americans are the source of the problem.

The protest grievance was begun by AIM as one of many problems the organization was contesting for Native people. This occurred when Belle-court and the AIM pan-Indian agenda for Native American sovereignty he represented was given a chance to speak to the UI campus during the height of the Native American Red Power movement protest actions across the country (Cornell 1988:150). Here, the claims makers saw an opening of political opportunity and evaluated the possible responses of power holders to AIM's contentions, and AIM decided it was worth the risk to make a statement about the practice of dancing Indian mascots and Native American-White relations. To appease AIM's initial criticism, the University removed the symbol of Chief Illiniwek from its letterhead stationery also in that year (Teters, *The Illio* 1975:155).

The popular, social, political, and economic culture of the UI, the Campustown area, and the cities of Urbana and Champaign, and to some extent the state of Illinois as well are linked together under the canopy of cultural hegemony. This is one that makes icons out of things Indian and institution-alizes the conglomerated mythology of the Fighting Illini as reality for public display and consumption. The influence of the debate and of its various positions, have small and concentrated pockets of support in the immediate geographic area around the University. Also, across the state from such a legacy of "playing Indian" at UI that it is reflective of a larger social system that is class-based/post-secondary education/elite that reveals itself in other areas of status and power such as State government, the US Senate, and Illinois State's Supreme Court. The shadow cast by the University mascot, Chief Illiniwek, is long across the prairies and rolling lands of Illinois and indirectly touches many more interests in the discourse. For as activist Char-lene Teters has observed university graduates "go on to positions of power in government and make decisions based on" this inaccurate information (Spin-del 2000:163).

The near-complete saturation of Illinois public life in regard to the recog-nition of the mascot is very often manipulated by the alumni of the state's flagship institution who serve in capacities to influence the political mean-ings of the mascot for the state's population.

> Almost every segment of this community including the Governor, you know, who would issue statements from his office. "Well, hell, I love the mascot. I would even get dressed up and wear war paint myself," you know, that kind of stuff. (Teters interview 2003)

I really hadn't had taken much notice to what extent these mascots are imbedded in mainstream culture here. So I didn't realize the extent to which it was deeply imbedded in the culture. And that shocked me, you know, the kind of resistance that people had to change and how conservative this community not the university community per say, but Illinois as a state outside of the university, was so wedded to this emotion attached to the symbol really surprised me. (Farnell interview 2002)

Mascot performances are often compared to "black-face" mockery in terms of differences in skin color and cultural modes, for white males whom become involved in mimicking blacks and Native peoples, do so in order to establish a personal and social hierarchy of power through mimicry.

Our counseling center pointed out the grave psychological impact this has not only on Native American students here, but on many of the students of color here and that it was causing some problems and that students have left campus because of this. (Kaufman interview 2002)

The effect of such imagery effects adults as well as children in terms of self-esteem in regards to such images displayed.

Because of the Chief, the campus is a pretty hostile environment for Native students that if they can pass as white or Latino they will do so. I thought, "Goodness," you know, "if that is not oppression, what is? A Native person can't be who they are on campus, that is awful." (Farnell interview 2002)

This political entrenchment reifies the power associated with the ability to define and present the mascot in frames the UI finds comforting to them.

It has to be taught to you and it is something that the university promotes. I think it is a big mistake for the university to keep promoting it. Obviously, I think there is a lot of people here that would like to get rid of it even in the administration, and they don't quite know how to. There is this huge tension and there is so much resistance on both sides that they don't quite know how to proceed, . . . but the Chief is definitely not going to work out in the long run—it's not a good way to proceed. (Spindel interview 2002)

The investment of the board of trustees (BOTs) to the mascot is shown in the reactionary defensive modes of discourse which the UI uses to define itself in the debate. It is a matter of power in terms of policy that the BOTs tried to maintain.

Here we are at an academic institution and there was refusal by the academic institution itself by the administration to even talk about an issue that was a major concern to the campus and that was not, in my mind, a very constructive way for an educational institution to refuse to engage in discourse on an issue of a concern to the campus and an educational concern. (Kaufman inteview 2002)

An internal study recommended that the UI retire its race-based mascot in order to promote a positive learning environment as well as to enhance the diversity of the campus population and inclusiveness of its educational mission and goals (Gehrt 1993:1). This would not only affect student financial aid but also receipt of research grants for academic endeavors at the UI (Kaufman interview 2002). Research monies would be jeopardized and the loss of such funding could essentially halt the UI in its tracks in regard to the situation. This could even affect the athletic programs that the university find so hallowed and important.

> They wrote a report which I think was about 40 pages long and about 30 of those pages was a condemnation of the University of Illinois for lack of integrity on this issue and its failure to deal with this issue in a constructive way. (Kaufman interview 2002)

> But the board of trustees totally ignored it. A democratically elected faculty senate of the university has asked administration to get rid of this symbol. So here was the voice of the campus saying, "Get rid of it." The board of trustees . . . didn't respond. In fact, all we got were sort of veiled threats that we were interfering with trustee business and we had no business speaking out on these kinds of issues at all. It was incredible. (Farnell interview 2002)

Next in this process is an escalation of the stakes and actions. In the University of Illinois case, it was the arrival of Charlene Teters to the UI campus. With the actions of Ms. Teters against the mascot, the level of visibility on the part of the anti-Chief campaign became much more national in visibility with the increased intensity of the reactions of University of Illinois that had supported the Chief mascot. The price of the resistant pro-mascot stance by the university in the discourse had become visibly realized as more public pressure began to escalate and with it a reputation as a place of notoriety on the national level of the debate by being recognized as a most resistant site of contention.

Protest became much more visible due to the actions of one woman. A sense of personal outrage to the mascot and the UI by Charlene Teters motivated her to act after she and her children witnessed the dancing mascot performance at a UI basketball game (*In Whose Honor?* 1997). In seeing the psychological hurt upon her children right happen before her eyes, she began to fight for the dignity of her children, not necessarily for her own anger at the dancing mascot but because her children's sense of self-esteem had suffered a blow by this public display of things Indian at the hands of the neo-Fighting Illini in the cites of Champaign-Urbana.

Once it became clear to me that it was undermining their self-esteem and it became very clear to me when I took them to the game. Once I saw it, it is like the stuff that I was tolerating myself, you know, just turned into this incredible, you know, I was just angry, angry at myself because we internalize so much. All of us do we witness things all of the time and we just internalize it. And we are told to tolerate it and we do, we tolerate all kinds of stuff. It was at that time that I became really committed and because of what I was seeing in my children. That, you know, they were sinking in their seats, they were humiliated, but when they could verbalize it. And they couldn't really verbalize it there while we were in the environment. (Teters interview 2003)

From this, Teters tells that people "were constantly trying to fight with her son in his school," and that her daughter "tried to become invisible" and deny her heritage (Chugurupati 1990:4).

My daughter did not say this when we were there, but after we left, after we were gone a couple of years, [she] could verbalize then which she could not when we were there that she felt close to suicide. So, you know, it is like, you know, whew, you know, there was so much more going on inside them that I wasn't even aware of really. (Teters interview 2003)

For her, this raised the stakes in the debate and made it personal. The inequality of the presumed power relationship between the pro- and anti-mascot groups involved in the debate "expressed in language of strong moral arguments" (Rose 2000:20). The subordinate side of the argument then becomes recognized and legitimate via acknowledgement by the power holder's superior position in the debate. It is in a context where the elite seek to retain "the ideology of the normative hegemony" (Tarrow 1977:76).

Teters did not fit within the "normative hegemony" of the pro-mascot camp. For one, she is a traditional dancer. This is how she sees the "core of her identity" (Chugurupati 1990:9). She was appalled at what was being offered as "authentic" Native dance performed by the Chief impersonator. This insider status of being a dancer gives Teters the expertise to evaluate the performance and judge the traditional validity of the routine. Her traditional values are what she is trying to maintain through her struggle. Another difference is that she is an artist, and she draws her subjects from her experiences in a traditional cultural upbringing through her artwork. This is how she is able to work through the being "treated poorly" and from being "shunned a lot" by the pro-mascot camp (Chugurupati 1990:9).

I clearly was being targeted within the community by people. They knew me, knew my face. I was in the paper and it wasn't very flattering. The media in the beginning was really about, it was a tool used to make me look stupid and ridiculous. (Teters interview 2003)

The actions from Teters's initiative at the University of Illinois led to other protests at other sites where Native American-based mascots, logos, and names were in use in high profile events.

> Because that was like '89, '90. We had created kind of this media phenomena around us. Which then became the catalyst for all of these other little fires that were going on all over the country. Which, you know, so it was, you know, so as much as the media was targeting me as a person, in the beginning. I got really good at using the media, you know, once I understood kind of how they operated. (Teters interview 2003)

Charlene Teters's protests caused the University of Illinois to step back from its official stance on the mascot issue and to reevaluate its own criteria of the legitimacy of the dancing Indian mascot.

> But when I started to bring people to campus, you know, as an organization, a student organization, we started to not only do the front line stuff while we are standing outside of games, we started to bring in speakers. So, you know, Vernon Bellecourt and Clyde [Bellecourt], and Michael Haney. Let me see who else. Wilma Mankiller was there. Gee, we brought a lot of people there to kind of speak on campus. It was kind of our effort to see us as something other than sort of these romantic, you know, in the past feathered dancing singing people. You know that we had our own, you know, educators, you know, we had, you know, lawyers we had doctors, you know. It was about trying to put another face to who we are as people. And we did an incredible job. I talk about "we" the organizations, Native American Students for Progress. To really filling the void in terms of people's understanding of who Native people and we were of course, we got really good at finding funds within the institution within the university's system. Through the student organization and we formed actually several organizations Native American Students for Progress, which was the Native voice on campus and we were always tiny. (Teters interview 2003)

There have been attempts in the past to establish a Native American presence on the UI campus: the most recent is the Red Roots student organization. This has been the most viable of the Native American student campus-based initiatives, founded in 1994 by UI Native American students (Reese interview 2002). Others include the National Coalition on Racism in Sports and Media, the Coalition Against Indian Racism, the Native American Students, Staff, and Faculty for Progress, Citizens for the American Indian Movement, and the Alumni Against Racist Mascots. Some or all formed in direct response to the UI pro-mascot stance over the length of the discourse. These localized campus-based as well as national level groups tried through the immediate circumstances at hand at the University of Illinois to build some national level of consensus on the issue and, in turn, direct or shape the debate for their side of the discourse.

These attempts have been short-lived because the turnover within some of these college student ranks is imminent with people graduating and leaving the UI for other places. Dr. Debbie Reese commented that often she found it hard to sustain the few Native students in attendance to join an organization and keep it going. When she arrived in Champaign-Urbana, there were fifteen or so "tribally enrolled, strongly Native people" (Reese interview 2002). Reese also commented that one of the fifteen had left UI because "it got too intense" for her. Reese reported the woman did come back, but approached one of her professors to speak about not letting others know she is a Native person. The woman did not want to attract attention to herself in the debate at UI. Reese felt that some students did not want to bring attention to their selves and become lightning rods for their opinions because such attention brought undo pressure on them. This woman hid her identity for the remainder of her time at UI (Reese interview 2002).

The Native American student group and its supporters had often been realized by the UI administration as a pariah, like an unwanted, unappreciated guest that simply cannot be rushed out of the dance because it is a member of the UI community. The student club was a part of the campus organizations and was a part of the debate however physically small in number it was in the past.

> At the time there were about 15 students and they were all from across the country and each one of them had the same story which was basically that they did not know what it was going to be like when they came here. And then, we all have the same story that people just can't believe that you are really Indian because you don't dress like the mascot, that you drive a car and live in a house. All that stuff that seems totally stupid. So, if you are not going to appear in a way that they want you to appear then they don't want you. (Reese interview 2002)

Charlene Teters's stand against the University of Illinois and its mascot brought the contemporary debate onto the national stage and prompted the recent changes in policy that some institutions have followed in retiring these particular displays of faux Native American cultural modes. It was her actions that serve as a linchpin in the matter, the debate now moving out into the national level of discourse arising from her one-person protests at UI.

Activists continue today to challenge stereotypes and exploitation of Native Americans by protesting the use of Indian mascots by athletic teams, and the dramatic growth in the number and variety of organizations designed to represent their interests.[9] The rise of Native peoples' protests has a distinct political and economic character that has mobilized urban and reservation members to use politics and the media to ensure that their grievances and demands are heard. Some observers feel the result is that overall, ethnic groups like Native Americans do not integrate into the American society and economy individually, but enter into the mainstream of American society as a people, and in particular as communities of people (Josephy, Nagel, and Johnson 1999:9).

This chorus of Native voice and their supporters speak of the factors of the frontier in regard to the influence of place and time on the debate with such comments made by the Illinois state governor, the SHs principal, and the Syracuse community supporting mascot presentations and displays. Because of the physical locations and the influence of colonialism on the discourse comments about the ownership and appropriateness of mascots is underscored by the disregard for the collective Native Americans speaking out against the practice. In terms of masculinity, the Native voice tells of prevalence of chiefs as mascots. White American males seek out other male positions of visibility or authority in order to negotiate their place in particular spaces of colonialism. Men seek even tacit support from these Other men, as they are being colonized by the former. Whiteness is critiqued by the chorus in that it is through power that whiteness reifies itself in terms of what it is and what it is not as it is compared and contrasted with the idealized Indian presented as a mascot. These three parameters of the research establish the bounds in which white American males construct Indian-ness in order to define themselves and their place in history and identity. The three frames show that these multitude of processes are available and fluid as they move about to define place, masculinity, and whiteness.

The Native American voice is encountered on all levels of the mascot discourse. The personal nature of the exploitation of these peoples and their societies and cultural displays is an element that serves to connect the different strata of the issue. The issue and self-worth of Native American youth is shared by the case study sites. Taking actions for social justice for Native Americans is shared, too. One difference of the examples is in the scope or scale in which the protest actions and voices are heard by the mainstream, and to which degree they are made visible. For example, Sue John's actions were highly focused on a specific group of students and on a particular Native American people. Doug George-Kanentiio's contentions had an effect on the central New York region and the fan base of the SU athletics teams. Charlene Teters's efforts became national in scope because she was in proximity to the then-second largest media market in the country. Her visibility of cause was enhanced by her actions occurring with literal earshot of Chicago. Her protest acts became news-item worthy and her story was given publicity.

The arguments Native Americans have made about the harm mascots can precipitate upon Native American peoples has been greatly studied and detailed. Some of these issues have been voiced by the consultants above. Though issues about ethnocized mascots of Native Americans is a more modern context of their relationship, the images of the constructed Indian have been around from contact with the European. The stoic silent image of the Indian Other has been the preferred representation of this other being by white American males. In contentions over mascots and how they are displayed for the public gaze, Native Americans are often caricatured beyond physical and cultural recognition for these consumable visible presentations. The voices that have been contextualized with one another reflect each other, and yet, still carry a quality of individuality about each, and, that taken together they collectively define the arguments for the whole of them. One it is hoped that such voices will not need to be heard above the din any more as the Indian-as-mascot will fade away and Native Americans will be dealt with in a much more mature and equal process; one that has moved on from difference and issues of power in regard to difference. The silencing of the Native voice over that matter will go far along the way in measuring the acceptance of Native Americans as a holistic comprehensive reality of their people by the mainstream.

Conclusion

In reviewing the research in terms of Native American–based mascots as they are perceived by American white males, it is clear that the parameters of this constructed Indian-ness are multiple and varied. While the reality of Native Americans and their everyday circumstances are acknowledged in varying degrees, the idealized symbol of the Indian-as-mascot is the preferred version that is welcomed into the *interior* of mainstream popular culture's domicile (Deloria 1998:58). The real Native American is thus relegated to the exterior of this realm, once again an outsider in their own historic lands and cultural spaces.

It is within these appropriated cultural spaces that the idealized Indian exists. It is in the betwixt and between places that the American white male controls the defining of those spaces in regard to identity and power. Mascots are located between the perceived reality and fantasy of the American white male imagination, the idea of the Indian moves about these places, touching upon them as islands in the debate, between the constructions of nationalism, race and ethnicity, economic, and sociocultural terrains. The tours the constructed ideal Indian travels about in these imagined regions are connected by contexts of time, history, entertainment, and consumption by and of the white male. It is in these spaces where the imagined Indian body provides a foil for the idealized American white male to compare and contrast itself in terms of masculine modes of representation.

In historical terms, the constructions of mascots are grounded in colonial experiences of conquest and conflict. War is the basic context of interaction between Red and White in the contestation for the country. The conflicts have become mythic in their recounting and repeated retellings. Mascots have then become invested in the myths of conquest and victory, containing the foundations of nationalism and American identity. Through time, mascots based on Native American people eventually have become alter-egos, secondary personas and identities which represent a connection to the past that romanticize colonial successes: the mascots figuratively embody the American Revolution. They are avatars of the founding of the American nation and the acquisition of the North American continent. In modernity, the mascots have been used as contemporary representations of identity and as forms of power. Native American-based mascots in their modern context are a means for role play which allows for American white males to express dystopian behavior as a form of playing Indian. The majority of mascot portrayals are also inventions of the twentieth century that serve to connect the modern with the mythic past.

The constructed Indian is an historic relic of the past relationships between Native and non-Native Americans. It is also a contemporary context that tells of the current relationship between the societies. The non-Native American mainstream audience sees Native Americans as predominantly caricatures of a different humanity, one that is viewed in the context of a colonized people. Sports team mascots grounded in this perspective confound the past and the present together in a singular discourse in order to use the ideals of the constructed Indian as a well-spring of racialized identity, historic experiences, and heroic maleness for white American men whom are invested in such ethnic notions of Indian-ness.

Though there has been a dearth of historic examples of Indian mascots, there has also been some positive movement in the direction away from their use in recent example. One case is the Victoria's Secret Lingerie Company and the use of a feathered headdress adorning one of their models. The model, Karlie Kloss, became the center of attention when she appeared on the catwalk in the adornment. The Native American community raised their collective voice to protest such an exhibition and the company edited out this portion of its television broadcast (ICTMN 2012). Also, the musical group No Doubt pulled a video of one of their performances where the band members were filmed playing cowboys and Indians for that performance. After being criticized for such a stunt by Native American critics the band reconsidered their production. The band agreed to pull the video from air, saying that because of the ethnic composition of their group, they did not mean to be insensitive to other minority groups by such a performance (ICTMN 2012). These actions, though, are quite small steps in relation to the mountainous volume of such reactionary presentations of idealized constructed Indianness. Still, these events could signal a shift in the way of the larger society's recognition of Native American concerns in regard to mascots and other forms of constructed Indian public performance and display.

One of the most significant measures taken had been by the National Collegiate Athletic Association (NCAA). In August 2005, under the direction of Myles Brand, the NCAA began a ban on such representations of

Native Americans, but only in the post-season and the policy prohibits such an institution from hosting post-season play (NCAA 2005). Its policy, however, leaves much room for a college or university to waffle through its rules for it allows some colleges and universities to continue to use racialized images because of an agreement between them and a Native tribe that condones the use of such a representation. The prime example of the use of this wiggle-room is that of the Florida State University and its relationship with the Seminole Tribe of Florida. The policy is majorly a paper tiger because it fails to enforce its stated mission by allowing some institutions to get away with using racialized imagery of Native American people. The NCAA fails to measure up to its own standards of the policy it espouses for its member institutions. It had been viewed as a step in the right direction in bettering the relationship between education institutions and Native Americans, but it has been a faulty misstep nonetheless. In order for the policy to be legitimate, the NCAA must realize the gap in its implementation and make the policy iron-clad in its use and application and make all members comply with the providing of an educational learning environment free of the potential of hostile environments and abusive practices. This context of the mascot debate is a matter of civil rights issues which are at the heart of such public displays which make entertainment of a group of people. Other academic institutions that have been able to walk through the policy gap are the University of Utah, the College of William and Mary, and Mississippi College. Here, the Running Utes, the Tribe, and Choctaws still have a place in higher education.

Since it is easier to make a rule and enact it in terms of a higher desired goal, it takes much more time for society to acquiesce to policy changes. No one knows how long such a temporal context may have to be put into complete practice and be active for it to become commonplace in Red-White relations and understanding. Mascots can be legislated away but its shadow still cast a long pall over ideas and intentions of social relationships between American white males and the Native Americans. The legacy of colonialism, of winners and losers in a greater nationalistic sense, still affects the way Native and non-Native peoples realize each other.

As I have reviewed this position taken by the NCAA it is a case of double-speak in which the NCAA seeks to confront race while it condones the use of such practices by select member institutions that have been able to rebuff the organization to get their way and ignore the policy. It is again an example of the Native voice being subsumed in the discourse by more powerful and influential actors that had become resistant to issues concerning the social justice concerns of Native Americans. Native Americans had once again become secondary props in the debate even when speaking out on issues that concern them, using their own voices to make such statements.

This contention however, seems to be problematic with the cases of the UND and the FSU. As Native voices have proclaimed a unified front against the use of race in creating mascots, logos and nicknames, these two examples confound the notion of consensus against constructed Indian-ness. In the light of the Seminole Nation supporting FSU and the Red Lake and Spirit Lake communities of Lakota/Sioux split over the UND's use of the Fighting Sioux name and logo, the picture of Native Americans and their relation to racialized mascots of them has become muddied.

Cultural critics, educators, and psychologists such as Harjo, Baca, Pewe-wardy, and Fryberg, and others point to the damage that can be brought upon Native American youth exposed to environments where Indian mascots are a part of entertainment and a mocking public display of their cultures and peoples. Over time, such exposure can have an effect on self-esteem, self-worth, and identity for this group of young people. The use of such iconic representations of Native Americans couched in racism is a potentially insidious use of American popular culture upon these people. A part of this concern is that such images and ideas can become accepted by these youths as a part of a form of power in which internalized institutionalized racism is the result of such experiences.

Following this line of critique, the racism where whiteness is grounded through the body of the Indian is that which has been commodified by the example of FSU and the Seminole Nation. This is a context of the friendly Noble Savage who is used by the white hero and willingly sacrifices his Noble self so that the white hero may succeed and therefore leave the good dead Indian behind in form, but carrying the idealized memory of his sacrifice forward. The idealized memory is the one which grounds the persona of Seminole chief Osceola into the present as a flaming war lance-toting, mounted warrior. Bedecked in authentic Seminole produced attire of predominantly red and yellow/garnet and gold, this contemporary Noble Savage rendition serves the FSU community as a caricatured amalgam of Plains and Seminole based notions of Indian-ness.

Likewise, the UND uses the idea of the Noble Savage to ground its version of the mascot in the historic experiences of whites with the Lakota people of the Dakotas. The Lakota hunted the buffalo, fought life-and-death conflicts with European/American settlers, and had populated the lands on which the UND now sits. This historic connection is one that serves this site as a legitimate use of the idealized Indian as a mascot icon. In this example the Chippewa artist and UND alumnus Bennett Brien had been placed in the role of the compliant friendly Indian, the helpmate of the white hero. It is Brien's labor that provided the university with the image of Fighting Sioux that supporters had rallied around in order to preserve constructed Indian-ness at this place. White masculinity becomes embedded in this context and wears the idealized Indian logo as a mask.

This trend of Native Americans whom are accepting of mascots as representations of their peoples and cultures tells of the level of the factor of internalized institutional racism upon Native Americans. The acceptance of such ideas of indigenous peoples by their own community is a marker of the power of this practice of acculturation and assimilation. Since mascots of athletics teams are most often tied to institutional education, mascots are an outgrowth of the boarding school mission of Richard H. Pratt's stated goal to "kill the Indian in him, and save the man" (Pratt 1892). Raciailized mascot representations are embedded with the historic experiences and cultural generalizations of the Indian. The historical contexts of the frontier inform the construction of mascots in terms of the past relationships of colonization and the dispossession of the Native peoples for the land. Here, past colonial history and nation-building processes are brought into the present by Indian mascots. In this critical frame, the frontier thus is still an active and vigorous context of Native and white relations.

In regard to the accepting of mascot imagery as a form of Native American identity, it is also a form of cultural reappropriation by Native Americans. As a factor of a context of political economy, the reclaiming of race-based imagery incorporates and accepts such ideas as it defies constructed Indian-ness. The use of American popular culture notions of Indian ethnicity creates images such as the profiled countenances of the Indian male such as the FSU logo of Osceola, the Chicago Blackhawk's use of Chief Blackhawk, and the UND's use of the Brien creation of Lakota manliness as a variety of Fighting Sioux. Since many of the ideas of authentic Native American men make it to the public's gaze, the re-appropriation of such ready-made images are used by Native individuals to self-identify, to make claims in a public space, as a Native American. The consumption of these images by Native Americans connects them to larger capital systems which are appreciably much bigger than the reservation and other Native communities on which these consumers reside. Other accessories of "race" or ethnic notion include feathers, painted designs, war-shields, and weaponry and are represented in these constructed images.

The availability of these types of images of Indian-ness provides for a context of recognition and visibility for the larger consumer public which are identifiable of things Indian. These images then become the items which Native Americans consume to use as a form of Native identity construction. As Native peoples reappropriate white imagery of what whites think Indians are as represented by mascots, Native people use them as a resistant frame to turn constructed Indian-ness back into a context of Native-ness, using it as a process of self-identity through which they are taking back control. It is a dynamic process in which the two groups are engaged. This cultural tug-of-war is one context that mascots and the larger dynamics of Native and non-Native relations can be evaluated. Though it is largely a symbolic, or at least grounded in symbols, argument among two sides, it is a highly emotional and charged discourse that keeps it in the public gaze and it is one of the most visible issues that whites know of Native people, especially when the discourse is centered by encountering the debate through sports as an entertainment format and as a popular culture icon for this audience.

This form of entertainment and the value for popular culture construction it holds for the audience where the Indian desired is an idealized Indian which symbolizes the conquest of a wild, empty land is also for making trophies of Native America and Native Americans. In this context, the winner must have spoils to have earned. The Native American corpus is that trophy, is that bloodied, red-stained spoil that was a way to tally the measure of colonial enterprise success in North America. As a relic of the colonial period of European interests in North America, the marker, the reddened skin taken from the body of a slain Native American makes a commodity of Native Americans, more especially the dead ones. The Frontier is where this bounty was encountered, though the frontier's location is a secondary concern because the entire continent at one time or another was the frontier, as it is for the boundaries of this historical place are fluid and liminal, the political contours of it shifting along with the changing currents the mascot debate takes.

As has been discussed, the land becomes one way to measure the success of the colonial effort to establish a new nation. However, the West or the Frontier has been a continuous process, one that did not climax in the nineteenth century. Patricia Nelson Limerick argues that the conquering process of colonialism is ever continuing (1987), and brings the frontier boundary with itself, dragging it through historic contexts into the present. In this particular context, it is a self-generating process. It is one that verifies itself when claiming real or imagined spaces. This follows Richard Drinnon's thesis offered in his text *Facing West: The Metaphysics of Indian-Hating and Empire Building* (1980), that the idea of the "Indian" travels along this border construct, precipitating the Indian Other wherever different peoples become encountered in the colonial and imperialist expansion of national interests beyond one's national boundaries. According to this, "Indians" are met wherever the West treads on new ground.

In terms of the Frontier-as-Place critical frame, Native Americans reside on the far side of the imagined boundary of the frontier, beyond a certain recognized distance or space. The Noble Savage lives inside of the boundary, but at the furthest edge of it. The Ignoble Savage clearly resides beyond this border and is constantly placed there, existing in the imagined wild reaches beyond civilization. This boundary is fluid and had changed its location through time in regard to the processes of colonialism and nation-building. Real Native Americans and the imagined villain embedded in the form of the Ignoble Savage are beyond the border of civilization, in the place Deloria speaks of as the exterior (1998). The romanticized Noble Savage is allowed within this boundary, however, although its distance from the center is consciously attended by American society's psyche: it is kept away at arm's length, where it can be accommodated and controlled in this schema of positionality.

As a place of historic experiences and where various nostalgias interact, the Frontier becomes a birthing site for the American Adam, too, a place where the archetype of American masculinity becomes constructed against the frontier, against a curtain of a means of the birthing a nation from the wilderness. The ability of the American physical body which can wrest a nation from an untamed land attests to the heroic masculinity of the American man.

The conditions of masculinity are ever-changing, too. At one point, it was valued and judged by the station of the man under evaluation. The male had to prove his competence by being responsible and being a mature adult. This meant having a career or profession, a home as a man's castle, and providing for and taking care of his family. Another context that was favored centered around physicality where a manly man could provide for through his labor, basing this on his individual ability and strength. The ability to personify primitive characteristics was another avenue of masculinity that was at one time shown favor. Here, the American man's ability to connect to different constructs of masculinity through a temporal frame, of the capability to connect the past with the present, conjoining a "natural" man with a contemporary man, such as it is embodied by the hero archetype. The Frontier man, the hero archetype man, or the self-made man, all of these representations of the idealized American male are examples of the individual components of the configurations of masculinity and its expressions for the public gaze. Masculinity is not a static representation of the American white male. It, too, is fluid and ever-changing, often incorporating past and present forms of it in myriad combinations that flow to match society's changing norms of men and masculinity.

Masculinity is a template for the mascot construction in frontier terms because the hero archetype is a character which walks in both spaces, Red and White. The Daniel Boone or Davy Crockett–like hero is the hunter who lives like the Indian on the frontier, in the wild, while maintaining his whiteness beneath the exterior of white Indian-ness costuming, of appearing as a wild Indian in dress. The hero archetype has also been called a hunter, one who preys upon Nature and the wild, killing it as a commodity for consumption. As well, the hero who hunts and preys upon the animals of the wilderness also becomes a hunter of the natural man living out there in the wilderness, the Indian Other is target for the hunter hero archetype. Making the wilderness safe by destroying the wild and all of its avatars shows the hunter as a ruthless savage hunting and killing the Indian of the wild. Whether as a Nick of the Woods or as John Moredock, the white male hunter was seen as necessary in order to meet the savage Indian on his terms out in the wild. The exalting of the hunter hero to mythic stature also elevated the destruction of the Indian by his hand as a necessary component of the archetype model of heroic behaviors.

In the grounding of gender in the masculinity construct of American white maleness, men necessarily measure each other's performance of masculinity. Men who perform the role of masculinity, or of its expectations by the viewers' evaluating the performance of men, consume the performance of it and then judge its value. In this context, masculinity, like playing Indian, is a role play of performance and can be thought of as "going Manly."

Gender as masculinity is also contextualized by violence, the main underpinning of colonialism. The incorporation of violence into this identity construct places it in several applications of it as a critical frame. Violence was used as a mode of protection against the wild things that lie beyond the pale of civilization. American white males used violence against the violent wilderness in order to protect their advance into that wilderness. Violence becomes justified when used against Native Americans in order to make claims on the land, to keep what had been taken and is now under the American white male's control. Also, violence was seen as necessary in terms of keeping the Indian under control. Violence against Native Americans was seen to be unavoidable in its use. It was seen as a means to dislocate the Native Americans from their own territories. Violent American white males have produced as well as have been products of violence, particularly when making claims of nationhood. If violence had been a part of the make-up of American males, then they perpetuate violence in order to maintain one part of their national identity.

As the masculine American man is constructed from elements of gender it is also contains the racial context of skin color as difference. The hero archetype as white man consumes the red Indian through means of the mascot representations through the imagined body of the white Indian. The white hero becomes "Indian" by wearing the literal skin of the Indian and so becomes an Indian via accessory and role play. Whiteness then is a costume, too. It is an outfit that allows the wearer access to forms of power which are used to ground identity construction of mascots from the Indian Other. This costume acts like chameleon skin, changing to adapt whiteness to fit inside of constructed Indian-ness.

The conditions and qualities of Whiteness provide for a multi-faceted construction of identity. As a precipitate of the power garnered through colonialism, Whiteness becomes a normative condition of race and ethnicity. Whiteness is used to evaluate the circumstance of the Other in relation to American white males as an over-riding standard that locates the Other in subordinate contexts. Whiteness is claimed to be an "invisible" quality because of the power it has surrounded itself within; it becomes invisible because it is subsumed in the power relations it expresses. This power of whiteness is ubiquitous in its ethnocentric context and is even expanded beyond nationalistic boundaries to include a globalized context of its expression as a hegemonic measure.

Whiteness has qualities which are overlain the idea of the Indian. Mascots facilitate this process by being a puppet to the whims of white males as it is used as entertainment. As a racialized spectacle of difference, the mascot is manipulated into various positions and locations that represent the Indian body being directed by white ideas of Indian-ness. Whiteness in the costume of Redness is a form of power that allows for differentiating identity through role play. The role play becomes the vehicle for cultural appropriation by American white males.

Whiteness fills the spaces between Native and non-Native in Western/ American society to produce a hegemonic preference of it that looks at whiteness as a color to cover over difference, and to act as a white canvas on which the placing of difference can become visualized through imagery that defines it. The glossed-over whiteness, though, still has contours and patterns, has ebbs and flows, has high and low points, and is as a textured surface that can disrupt the expression of such imagery which fills the white space because the "lumps" under the canvas cannot completely cover over the Indian Other. Thus the images produced from the white male hegemonic position are skewed and caricatured, following the popular notions of Indianness as a template for difference. Whiteness is thus the White Indian dressed in Indian costume and playing Indian as a mascot in a gate-keeping role play at entertainments that celebrate conquest and nationalistic narratives.

Performance is part of the construction of mascots. The pageantry, spectacle, and visual presentation of mascots are readily consumed by a viewing audience because of the exotic nature of the Indian in the mainstream imagination. The "live" nature of the performance contextualizes many aspects of the investments of mascot supporters by condensing them into a singular body. The white Indian-come-to-life is a vessel into which ideas such as identity, fictive kinship, nationalism, history, and nostalgia among a host of many other contexts are poured into its body. This analogy is similar to the idea of boarding schools' mission to "kill the Indian in him, and save the man" where the Native American's body is emptied of its original culture and knowledge and the hollow shell is then filled with Western American ideals producing an acceptable copy of the Indian-as-white male.

The context of authenticity is embedded in the mascot and its side-line display. The accessories of Indian-ness dress the body of the performer in order to visually display a legitimate lineal descent from the colonial past through the body of the idealized Indian mascot bringing the performance and its display into the contemporary moment. Feathers, paint, leather clothing, beads, and weaponry fulfill the expectations of presentation that define Indian-ness of American popular culture. Following the old saw about the way of defining what a duck is, i.e. if it walks like, talks like, and quacks like a duck, it must be a duck, so too this convention holds for defining what an Indian is: so, if it dresses like, dances like, and acts like an Indian, it must be one. As a gatekeeper, the side-line mascot is entertainment and leisure as it connects the past to the present, and is an alter-ego as the white Indian. It provides proof of the legitimacy of American white males to the land, nation, and to an identity in which to locate their individual selves.

Mascot representations reflect the success of nation-building by embodying the constructed ideas of conquered peoples, tamed wildernesses, historic touchstones, and contemporary expressions of the individual that when taken as a whole are collectively regarded as a set of nationalistic preferred readings of identity. In the transformation of the land into a nation, Native American-based mascots contain colonial contexts of conquest and control. Mascots, then, serve American white males as a way to represent the totality of the land and of things upon the land that have been conquered in the procurement of the West via Native America.

What has been learned by this research, what are the intersections and investments in mascots by white American males? Mascots are not the intertwined negotiations and mediations over time and place between Red and White cultures. Mascots are wholly white inventions of desired and loathed reflections of self in regard to the conquest of people and land, very few mascots are of indigenous origin and founding. Mascots have a generational context in terms of location and use by institutions which are localized by place and time. They are also compacted with paradoxes that range from expressions of sure power to neurotic uses of self-introspection, from friendly to hostile forms, from fear to fascination. Along the many points located on these axes, the particular reading of the mascot in context is contained within these perspectives of difference. In turn, these perspectives create and support spaces and distances of Whiteness in relation to located imaginings of the Native American-as-Indian Other. In the use of mascots to ground an identity of white American males, it too can be thought of as a coin with Redness on one side and Whiteness on the other side.

In the debate over the use of mascots, it is now known that mascots have negative effects on Native Americans, particularly on Native youth. However, this research has tried to shed light on the impact on white American males and their investment in mascots and their construction of self-identity. How have they incorporated this militant version of Indian-ness into their own make-up of the self? How has whiteness reinforced beliefs of conquest? The document tells of how whiteness reinforces white racialized notions of the Other. These ideas reinforce white notions of supremacy by seeming to place difference as a natural result of colonialism. How white men and boys have been influenced by a stereotype, a fiction created about Native

Americans and grounded through the Indian mascot, is an example of the power of identity when it is constructed through race and ethnicity.

In a final thought on the use of racialized mascots based on the lives and social modes of Native American peoples, to end such displays can take some sort of policy or directive to retire mascots based on living, real human beings. Native Americans are the only existing socio-cultural group who are represented as mascots because mascots have been idealized through popular cultural notions. Human beings are represented by mascots, and these are typically apolitical such as Commodores, Engineers, Patriots, Colonials, Cowboys, or even Presidents. However, these are roles, occupations, or historic contexts of peoples and institutions. Native Americans are living beings who become politicized because of the competitive and combative experiences in which their idealizations by the larger American society are grounded. Native Americans as represented by the idealized Indian, then become two-dimensional mascots, losing their humanity as part of the construct, whereas three-dimensional people have a much harder time in becoming folded into the body that the mascot represents. It is easier to manipulate an idea rather than real people who may complain about being handled and regarded in such a fashion. This will (hopefully) over time be one way to decrease the perceived spaces and distances between Red and White cultures.

Notes

CONTESTING CONSTRUCTED INDIAN-NESS

1. This a pseudonym assigned to this student for anonymity.
2. Such regalia is usually reserved for traditional and Western or pow-wow styled dance performers, they investing much time into their outfits and accessories.
3. This critical frame is building upon the category of white studies. Whiteness as an ethnicity like Native American studies or Latino studies is grounded in ethnicity as a critiquing frame. White studies looks at white people and their cultures with this critical lens making the White Other in this case.
4. This context of savagery is off-set by the "hidden" aspect of the whiteness of the hero archetype, he being only accessorized to look like an Indian. His whiteness grounds him in civilization no matter how far his actions go into savagery.
5. Most mascot caricatures have been created by non-Native Americans to depict the popular cultural notions of Indian-ness as held by the American white male psyche.
6. The former contemporary rendition of the Indian head logo had been created by a Native American alumnus of the UND. This had been used by the pro-mascot camp as a justification to retain the mascot logo and the connection to the Fighting Sioux.
7. The possessors of these "voices" have a great deal of activist work for Native people and against constructed Indian mascots.
8. This act of consumption on the part of the viewing public is also an act of symbolic cannibalism. I view the buying of such associated sports team paraphernalia as one way to "own" an Indian, and by possessing it, the item or thing becomes emotionally consumed and internalized, ingested along with nostalgia.

1. THE FRONTIER AS PLACE/SPACE

1. The Native American corpus becomes the vessel in which the qualities of Noble and Ignoble Savagery reside.
2. The wild context of the unconquered land effects civilized man in a manner like it effects the Indian as it makes the civilized man act in a wild, uncontrolled fashion, makes him become a savage by leaving civilized behaviors behind at the boundary of the wilderness and civilization.

3. Like a flag planted at the farthest most reach of civilization, the settlers' progress was marked by such iconic symbols like the wagons that carried the families westward until they could go no farther.

4. Man Friday served Robinson Crusoe; Tonto served the Lone Ranger; Blue Back aided Henry Fonda's character, Gil Martin, in John Ford's 1939 film, *Drums Along the Mohawk*

5. From this Onondaga community looking northward, one can see Syracuse University sitting up on the hill, and though it is mere minutes driving from the Onondaga Nation, there are far greater distances between the two locations that exist in reality.

6. Zuppke had imagined this linguistic knowledge as the Illini Confederacy peoples had been driven out of the bounds of the state of Illinois in 1827, nearly a century before his proclamation.

7. The university has an alumnus who breeds the Appaloosas in order to have a ready supply of such horses and trains them to perform the on-field act. Currently, Renegade V is the horse on which the faux Chief Osceola rides onto the football field.

2. GENDER, MASCULINITY, AND MALE IDENTITY

1. It is in this construct that the spaces are created to show difference. Masculinity helps to ground the perceived physical distances and spaces between white males and the Indian Other.

2. The power of the hunter is reframed. Here it is the removal of the Indian male from the picture which leaves the Indian woman as a part of this equation. Here it is the Native American woman's body which is now the object of white male actions.

3. Masculinity becomes the performance of physicality. White males' physical appearance in this context uses the exterior to tell of the interior strength of the body.

4. As a hunter, the white masculine male holds the ultimate power over the body of the Indian. The hunter has the literal power of life and death in his control, and the fate of the Indian awaits its whim. The blood spilled in this context makes the hunter-as-white Indian red in color. This red can be cleansed off, though, with the hunter recovering his whiteness through his washing of the blood from his body.

5. Brien was in no way being taken advantage of because he was free-lancing commissions for his artwork. As Strinden pointed out, Brien made a painting for him and the idea of it becoming a logo gained its own momentum.

6. The bronze of Engelstad looks into the faces of the people coming into the facility as they arrive in the entrance. The sculpture stands on a small riser at the far wall of the main lobby floor space.

7. The topic began to dominate the agendas of tribal business and the issue also influenced tribal politics in terms of political platforms.

3. WHITE IDENTITY, WHITE IDEOLOGIES, AND CONDITIONS OF WHITENESS

1. The AAA set the guidelines for the field. This perspective clearly defines race as a social construct of power based on physical differences and has tried to move away from its use in describing humans. However, this concept is greatly packed and will take some time for it to leave the use of it in the discipline.

2. In this educational institution context, mascot sideline performers most frequently have been young white males. These youth have found the opportunity to play Indian a cherished college memory.

3. In the physical properties of white or as white light, this has the quality of reflecting all colors of white light. In following that white is nothing, as a blank space, white becomes some *thing* by reflecting back what it comes in contact with.

4. CONSTRUCTING THE NATIVE VOICE

1. The chorus of voices is intertwined and yet are as distinctive of one another. The arenas in which the different levels of voices become aired are also different, but they are connected through protest of the contentions of public displays of constructed Indian-ness.

2. The Seneca Nation of Indians has three territories which make up the lands of the SNI. They are the Oil Spring, Cattaraugus, and Allegany Reservations.

3. The "contracting" districts serve the local Native American student populations by providing educational services such as tutoring, cultural programming, setting goals and evaluating outcomes of the performances of the Native Americans students in attendance in the district.

4. The idea linking a Native American context to the Orangeman began in 1931 as a fiction story in a campus satire publication. Over the following forty-five years the story became a gospel to the university and its sports team boosters.

5. The ideas expressed by George-Kanentiio in his thoughts are now material items used by other institutions such as Native American housing and living space, Native American support staff and programs, and classes on Native American peoples. In New York State such initiatives have been taken up by Cornell University, the SUNY University at Buffalo, and Syracuse University.

6. The University of Miami (OH) Redskins have since become the RedHawks.

7. The Onondaga Chiefs must use reason and deliberation in their council meetings for as much as they represent the political interests of clan, community, and nation as determined by their clan mothers, they also serve as mediators of conflict resolution. Their decisions must benefit the nations of the Confederacy as a whole.

8. This bronze sculpture now resides in the Orange Grove section of the Syracuse University Quad. The bronze's contorted body highlights the Noble Savage qualities of the idealized constructed Indian. Kaisch had used a man from the Onondaga Nation to pose as the model for the statue's elements.

9. The University of Illinois has created a Native American studies program, as well as establishing Native American student housing, the addition of cultural programming, and faculty and staff.

Bibliography

Abernathy, David. "Saltine Warrior: Discard the Symbol of Racism," *The Daily Orange*, November 14, 1977.

Alumni News, Syracuse University, December 1978.

American Anthropological Association, "AAA Statement on Race," American Anthropological Association, 1998.

Baca, Lawrence R. "Native Images in Schools and the Racially Hostile Environment," *The Native American Mascot Controversy: A Handbook*, edited by C. Richard King, Lanham, MD: Scarecrow Press, 2010.

Baker, Kendall L. "Public Statement, January 12, 1993 [University of North Dakota, Sioux Nickname]," *Wicazo Sa Review* 9, 1 (1993): 67–71.

Banks, Serenity J. "'Fighting Sioux' Name Sees New Advocate in Protest: Thirty Years of Conflict and Still No Resolution," *Lakota Journal*, www.und.edu/org/bridges/banks.html.

Barrett, Joe. "University Loses Sioux Mascot War," *The Wall Street Journal*, April 10, 2010.

Basso, Keith H. *Wisdom Sits in Places: Landscape and Language among the Western Apache*, Albuquerque, NM: University of New Mexico Press, 1996.

Berkhofer Jr., Robert F., *The White Man's Indian: Images of the American Indian from Columbus to the Present*, New York: Vintage Books, 1978.

Bilharz, Joy. *The Allegany Senecas and Kinzua Dam: Forced Relocation through Two Generations*, Lincoln: The University of Nebraska Press, 1998.

Bird, S. Elizabeth. *Dressing In Feathers: The Construction of the Indian in American Popular Culture*, edited by S. Elizabeth Bird, Boulder, CO: Westview Press, 1998.

Black, Jason Edward. "The 'Mascotting' of Native America: Construction, Commodity, and Assimilation," *American Indian Quarterly* 26, 4 (2002): 605–22.

Brownstein, Andrew. "A Battle Over a Name in the Land of the Sioux," *The Chronicle of Higher Education* XLVII, 24 (February 23, 2001): 46–49.

Casey, Edward S. "How to Get from Space to Place in a Fairly Short Stretch of Time: Phenomenological Prolegomena," *Senses of Place*, eds., Steven Feld and Keith H. Basso, Santa Fe, NM: School of American Research, 1996, 13–52.

Castagno, Angelina E., and Stacey J. Lee. "Native Mascots and Ethnic Fraud in Higher Education: Using Tribal Critical Race Theory and the Interest Convergence Principle as an Analytic Tool," *The Native American Mascot Controversy: A Handbook*, edited by C. Richard King, Lanham, MD: Scarecrow Press, 2010.

Champagne, Denise M. "School Defending Its Warrior Mascot, Board Rejects State Suggestion to Change," *The Salamanca Press*, May 23, 2001, 1.

Chmiel, Renee. "Fighting Sioux Logo Designer Sad to See it Retired, UND Logo Artist Reacts to Retirement," WDAZ Television Channel 8, Grand Forks, ND, April 18, 2010.

Chugurupati, Sridhar. "Teters Tells the Tale of Struggle against the Chief," One on One, *The Daily Illini*, October 12, 1990, 4, 9.

Coffey, Thomas. "Saltine Warrior Fights Last Battle," *The Daily Orange*, March 2, 1978, 10.

Cornell, Stephen. *The Return of the Native: American Indian Political Resurgence*, Oxford: Oxford University Press, 1988.

Crouse, Robin. Personal interview, Seneca Nation of Indians Health Administration Offices, December 2, 2004.

Davey, Monica. "In Twist, Tribe Fights for College Nickname," *The New York Times*, December 8, 2009, A18.

Davis, Laurel. *The Swimsuit Issue and Sport: Hegemonic Masculinity in* Sports Illustrated," Albany, NY: SUNY Press, 1997.

Deloria, Philip J. *Playing Indian*, New Haven, CT: Yale University Press, 1998.

Drinnon, Richard. *Facing West: The Metaphysics of Indian-Hating and Empire-Building*, Minneapolis: University of Minnesota Press, 1980.

Dyer, Richard. *White*, London: Routledge Press, 1997.

Engelstad, Ralph. "A $100-Million Donor's Ultimatum," letter excerpted in *The Chronicle of Higher Education* XLVII, 24 (February 24, 2001): 47.

Fabian, Johannes. *Time and the Other: How Anthropology Makes Its Object*, New York: Columbia University Press, 2002.

Farnell, Brenda. Personal interview, University of Illinois, February 21, 2002.

Ferber, Abby L. *White Man Falling: Race, Gender, and White Supremacy*, Lanham, MD: Rowman & Littlefield Publishers, Inc., 1998.

Florio, Gwen. "Think Fighting Sioux Nickname Ban Ended Controversy? Wrong!" *The Buffalo Post*, April 17, 2010.

Foley, Douglas. *The Heartland Chronicles*, Philadelphia: University of Pennsylvania Press, 1995.

Foster, Thomas A. "Introduction," *New Men: Manliness in Early America*, edited by Thomas A. Foster, New York: New York University Press, 2011.

Gehrt, Trey. "Chief Banned from Floats," *The Daily Illini*, October 29, 1993, 1, 6.

George-Kanentiio, Doug. Personal interview, Syracuse University, September 19, 2002.

George-Kanentiio, Doug. Online interview, America On Line, Wednesday, August 25, 2004.

Grand Forks Herald, 1997.

Greene, Rayna. "The Tribe Called Wannabee: Playing Indian in America and Europe," *Folklore* 99 (1988): 30–55.

Harjo, Suzan Shown. "Note to Congress: Stop Shielding 'Indian' Mascots and Start Defending Indian People," *The Native American Mascot Controversy: A Handbook*, edited by C. Richard King, Lanham, MD: Scarecrow Press, 2010.

Helmberger, Pat. *Indians as Mascots in Minnesota Schools*, Burnsville: Friends of the Bill of Rights Foundation, 1999.

Heron, Tyler. Personal interview, Salamanca High School, April 19, 2002.

Hirschfelder, Arlene B. *American Indian Stereotypes in the World of Children: A Reader and Bibliography*, Lanham, MD: Scarecrow Press, 1982.

Honyoust, Dan. Personal interview, Syracuse University, October 17, 2002.

Horowitz, Helen Lefkowitz. *Campus Life: Undergraduate Cultures from the End of the Eighteenth Century to the Present*, Chicago: The University of Chicago Press, 1987.

Huff, Shelley R. Tribal Clerk, Seneca Nation of Indians, Regular Session of Tribal Council Resolution CN: R-05-12-01-24, May 12, 2001.

Huff, Wendy. Personal interview, SUNY Fredonia, Fredonia, NY, May 30, 2001.

Huhndorf, Shari M. *Going Native: Indians in the American Cultural Imagination*, Ithaca, NY: Cornell University Press, 2001.

In Whose Honor? American Indian Mascots in Sports. Documentary film, Dir.: Jay Rosenstein, New Day Films, Hohokus, NJ, 60 mins., 1997.

Indian Country Today Media Network. "No Doubt Pulls 'Looking Hot' Video and Issues Apology," November 3, 2012.

Indian Country Today Media Network. "Eastern Michigan University Brings Back Divisive Indian Logo to 'Honor its History, Pride,'" September 8, 2012.

Indian Country Today Media Network. "Here We Go Again: Victoria's Secret Angel Karlie Kloss Dons Headdress," November 8, 2012.

Iowa State University. "ISU Anthropology Professor Studying the Fighting Sioux Mascot Controversy," News Service, University Relations, Ames, Iowa, August 15, 2011, website: online@iastate.edu.

Johansen, Bruce. "Putting the Moccasin on the Other Foot: A Media History of the 'Fighting Whities,'" *The Native American Mascot Controversy: A Handbook*, edited by C. Richard King, Lanham, MD: Scarecrow Press, 2010.

John, Adrian. Personal interview, Seneca Nation of Indians Higher Education Program, April 19, 2002.

John, Sue. Personal interview, Salamanca High School, September 29, 2000.

John, Sue. Personal interview, Salamanca High School, May 31, 2001.

Johnson, Susan Lee. "'A Memory Sweet to Soldiers': The Significance of Gender in the History of the 'American West,'" *The Western Historical Quarterly* 24, 4 (November 1993): 495–517.

Josephy, Alvin M., Joane Nagel, and Troy Johnson, eds., *Red Power: The American Indian's Fight for Freedom*, Lincoln: University of Nebraska, 1999.

Kaufman, Stephen. Personal interview, University of Illinois, February 21, 2002.

Kimmel, Michael. *Manhood in America: A Cultural History*, New York: Oxford University Press, 2012.

King, C. Richard. "This Is Not an Indian: Situating Claims about Indianness in Sporting Worlds," *Journal of Sport and Social Issues* 28, 3 (2004): 3–10.

King, C. Richard. "Defensive Dialogues" *The Native American Mascot Controversy: A Handbook*, edited by C. Richard King, Lanham, MD: Scarecrow Press, 2010.

King, C. Richard, and Charles Fruehling Springwood. *Team Spirits: The Native American Mascots Controversy*, edited by C. Richard King and Charles Fruehling Springwood, Lincoln: University of Nebraska Press, 2001.

King, C. Richard, and Charles Fruehling Springwood. *Beyond The Cheers: Race as Spectacle in College Sport*, Albany: State University of New York Press, 2001.

Limerick, Patricia Nelson. *The Legacy of Conquest: The Unbroken Past of the American West*, W. W. Norton and Company, New York, 1987.

Lipsitz, George. *The Possessive Investment in Whiteness: How White People Profit From Identity Politics*, Philadelphia: Temple University Press, 1998.

Machamer, Ann Marie (Amber). "Last of the Mohicans, Braves, and Warriors: The End of American Indian Mascots in Los Angeles Public Schools," *Team Spirits: The Native American Mascots Controversy*, edited by C. Richard King and Charles Fruehling Springwood, Lincoln: University of Nebraska Press, 2001.

Masters, Bill. "Forgetting Tradition," *The Daily Orange*, February 16, 1978.

McCurdy, John Gilbert. "Gentlemen and Soldiers: Competing Visions of Manhood in Early Jamestown," *New Men: Manliness in Early America*, edited by Thomas A. Foster, New York: New York University Press, 2011.

McEwan, Patrick J., and Clive R. Belfield. "Native American Mascots and Alumni Giving," *The Native American Mascot Controversy: A Handbook*, edited by C. Richard King, Lanham, MD: Scarecrow Press, 2010.

Mechling, Jay. "Florida Seminoles and Marketing of the Last Frontier," *Dressing in Feathers: The Construction of the Indian in American Popular Culture*, edited by S. Elizabeth Bird, Boulder, CO: Westview Press, 1998.

Mihesuah, Devon A. *American Indians: Stereotypes and Realities*, Atlanta, GA: Clarity Press, 1996.

Mishkind, Marc E., Judith Rodin, Lisa R. Silberstein, and Ruth H. Striegel-Moore. "The Embodiment of Masculinity: Cultural, Psychological, and Behavioral Dimensions," *Changing Men: New Directions in Research on Men and Masculinity*, edited by Michael S. Kimmel, London: Sage Publications, 1987.

Munson, Barbara E. "Teach Then Respect Not Racism: Common Themes and Questions about the Use of 'Indian' Logos," *The Native American Mascot Controversy: A Handbook*, edited by C. Richard King, Lanham, MD: Scarecrow Press, 2010.

National Collegiate Athletics Association. Native American Mascot Policy—Status List, August 2005.

Newitz, Annalee. "White Savagery and Humiliation, or a New Racial Consciousness in the Media," *White Trash*, edited by Matt Wray and Annalee Newitz, New York: Routledge Press, 1997.

Newitz, Annalee, and Matt Wray. "Introduction," *White Trash*, edited by Matt Wray and Annalee Newitz, New York: Routledge Press, 1997.

O'Brien, Ann. Personal interview, Salamanca High School, April 19, 2002.

Onkwehonweneha. "Warrior: Based on a Lie," *The Daily Orange*, March 3, 1978.

Padilla, Howie. "Gift Causes Confusion in Logo Debate," *Dakota Student*, November 19, 1999.

Pasho, Kathy. "SU: Stand up," *The Syracuse Herald American*, February 26, 1978, p. 76.

Pearce, Roy Harvey. *Savagism and Civilization: A Study of the Indian and the American Mind*, Berkeley: University of Californian Press, 1988.

Penner, James. *Pinks, Pansies, and Punks: The Rhetoric of Masculinity in American Literary Culture*, Bloomington: Indiana University Press, 2011.

Pewewardy, Cornel D. "Playing Indian at Halftime: The Controversy over American Indian Mascots, Logos, and Nicknames," *The Clearing House* 77, 5 (2004): 180–85.

Pfeil, Fred. *White Guys: Studies in Postmodern Domination and Difference*, London: Verso Publishing, 1995.

Poe, Richard. *The Syracuse New Times*, 1978.

Pratt, Richard H. Official Report of the Nineteenth Annual Conference of Charities and Correction, (1892), 46–59. Reprinted in Richard H. Pratt, "The Advantages of Mixing Indians with Whites," *Americanizing the American Indians: Writings by the "Friends of the Indian" 1880–1900*, Cambridge, MA: Harvard University Press, 1973, 260–71.

Ralbovsky, Marty. "An Indian Affair: American Indian Students Concerned about Nicknames, Mascots in Sports," *The New York Times*, 1971, *American Indian Stereotypes in the World of Children: A Reader and Bibliography*, Arlene B. Hirschfelder, 1982.

Reese, Debbie. Personal interview, Urbana, Illinois, June 10, 2002.

Roediger, David R. *The Wages of Whiteness: Race and the Making of the American Working Class*, Rev. Ed., London: Verso, 1999.

Roediger, David. *How Race Survived U.S. History: From Settlement and Slavery to the Obama Phenomeno*n, London: Verso Press, 2008.

Rosaldo, Renato. *Culture and Truth: The Remaking of Social Analysis*, Boston: Beacon Press, 1989.

Rose, Fred. *Coalitions across the Class Divide: Lessons from the Labor, Peace, and Environmental Movements*, Ithaca, NY: Cornell University Press, 2000.

Rudolph, Frederick. *The American College & University: A History*, Athens: The University of Georgia Press, 1990.

Rychcik, John E., and David E. Edstrom. *80 Years of Excellence: Salamanca Football, Foundation-Tradition-Pride*, Salamanca: RJP Ready Print, 2001.

Saunders, Michael. "History of the Fighting Sioux Name at UND," American Indian Sports Team Mascots, http://aistm.org/und.htm.

Seneca Nation Education Department and Salamanca City Central School District, "Native American Educational Services," informational pamphlet, 2002.

Shefflin, Francis. "A Question of Pride," *The Daily Orange*, November 7, 1977.

Signore, Cheryl. Personal interview, Salamanca High School, December 3, 2004.

Slotkin, Richard. *Regeneration Through Violence: The Mythology of the American Frontier, 1600–1860*, Middletown, CT: Wesleyan University Press, 1973.

Smith, David. Personal interview, Syracuse University, June, 2005.

Smith-Rosenberg, Carroll. *This Violent Empire: The Birth of an American National Identity*, The Omohundro Institute of Early American History and Culture, Chapel Hill: The University of North Carolina Press, 2010.

Spindel, Carol. *Dancing at Halftime: Sports and the Controversy over American Indian Mascots*, New York: New York University Press, 2000.

Spindel, Carol. Personal interview, University of Illinois, February 18, 2002.

Springwood, Charles Fruehling. "'I'm Indian Too!': Claiming Native American Identity, Crafting Authority in Mascot Debates," *Journal of Sport and Social Issues* 28 (2004): 56.

Stashenko, Joel. "SU Loses a Legend," *The Daily Orange*, March 27, 1978.

Staurowsky, Ellen J. "Privilege at Play: On the Legal and Social Fictions that Sustain American Indian Sport Imagery," *Journal of Sport and Social Issues* 28 (2004): 11.

Staurowsky, Ellen J. "American Indian Imagery and the Miseducation of America," *The Native American Mascot Controversy: A Handbook*, edited by C. Richard King, Lanham, MD: Scarecrow Press, 2010.

Strain, Christopher B. *Reload: Rethinking Violence in American Life*, Nashville, TN: Vanderbilt University Press, 2010.

Syrett, Nicholas L. *The Company He Keeps: A History of White College Fraternities*, Chapel Hill: The University of North Carolina Press, 2009.

Tarrow, Sidney. Between Center and Periphery: Grassroots Politicians in Italy and France, New Haven, CT: Yale University Press, 1977.

Tarrow, Sidney. *Power in Movement: Social Movements, Collective Action and Politics*, Cambridge: Cambridge University Press, 1994.

Taussig, Michael. *Mimesis and Alterity: A Particular History of the Senses*, New York: Routledge, 1992.

Taylor, Michael. Native American Images as Sports Team Mascots: From Chief Wahoo to Chief Illiniwek, Dissertation, UMI Dissertation Services, Ann Arbor, 2005.

Taylor, Michael. "The Salamanca Warriors: A Case Study of an 'Exception to the Rule,'" *Journal of Anthropological Research* 67, 2 (2011): 245–65.

Teters, Charlene. Personal interview, Cornell University, Ithaca, April 11, 2003.

Teters, Charlene. www.charleneteters.com. *The Illio*, 1975.

The *Syracuse Post Standard*. September Monday Morning Quarterback, "Orange's 'Wimpy' Warrior Must Go," *The Syracuse Post Standard*, September 15, 1980.

Thomas, David Hurst. *Skull Wars: Kennewick Man, Archeology, and the Battle for Native American Identity*, New York: Basic Books, 2000.

Tucker, James. "Remove Name," *The Syracuse Herald Journal*, February 22, 1978, 12.

University of Illinois. "Chief Illiniwek Will No Longer Perform," news release, Office of University Relations, February 16, 2007, 1.

University of North Dakota. Official website, 2012.

University of North Dakota Indian Association. "History," University of North Dakota website, 2012.

Vecchiarella, April M. City Clerk, City of Salamanca Council Chambers Resolution in Support of Keeping "Warriors" at the High School, June 1, 2001.

Wahlberg, David Carl. "Strategies for Making Team Identity Change," *The Native American Mascot Controversy: A Handbook*, edited by C. Richard King, Lanham, MD: Scarecrow Press, 2010.

Waite, Todd. Personal interview, Seneca Nation of Indians Higher Education Offices, December 2, 2004.

Wallace, Paul A. W. *The White Roots of Peace*, Saranac Lake: The Chauncy Press, 1986.

Ward, Mark J. Letter to NYSED Commissioner Mills, Salamanca City Central School District, June 28, 2001.

Ward, Mark J. Personal interview, Salamanca High School, October 26, 2001.

"What's In a Name?" *The Salamanca Press*, Wednesday, May 23, 2001, 1.

White, Donald. Letter in response to Commissioner Mills, SNI Department of Education, May 30, 2001, 1, 2.

White, Donald. Personal interview, Seneca Nation of Indians Higher Education Program, April 19, 2002.

Yonker, Diane. Salamanca City Central School District Board of Education Meeting Resolution, May 22, 2001.

SELECTED ADDITIONAL BIBLIOGRAPHY

Coward, John C. *The Newspaper Indian: Native American Identity in the Press, 1820–1890*, Urbana: University of Illinois Press, 1999.

Farnell, Brenda. "The Fancy Dance of Racializing Discourse," *Journal of Sport and Social Issues* 28 (2004): 30.

Ferber, Abby L., and Michael S. Kimmel. "'White Men are this Nation': Right-Wing Militias and the Restoration of Rural American Masculinity," *Home-Grown Hate: Gender and Organized Racism*, edited by Abby L. Ferber, New York: Routledge, 2004.

Jensen, Robert. "What the 'Fighting Sioux' Tells Us about White People," *The Native American Mascot Controversy: A Handbook*, edited by C. Richard King, Lanham, MD: Scarecrow Press, 2010.

Kaplan, Amy. "Romancing the Empire: The Embodiment of American Masculinity in the Popular Historical Novel of the 1890s," *American Literary History* 2, 4 (Winter 1990): 659–90.

King, C. Richard. "Preoccupations and Prejudices: Reflections on the Study of Sports Imagery," *Anthropologica* 46, 1 (2004): 29–36.

Rehling, Nicola. *Extra-Ordinary Men: White Heterosexual Masculinity in Contemporary Popular Cinema*, Lanham, MD: Lexington Books, 2009.

Stedman, Raymond William. *Shadows of the Indian: Stereotypes in American Culture*, Norman: University of Oklahoma Press, 1982.

Index

Abernathy, David, 105
academic institutions: and alumni support of mascots, 80–81; as legitimizing agency for mascots, 75; racism of, 78, 79–80. *See also specific institutions*
alumni, support of mascots by, 80–81
American Anthropological Association (AAA), 74
American Indian Movement (AIM), 109–110. *See also* protests
American Indians, 102; as component of whites' identity, 83; co-opted as mascots, 9; as critics of mascots, 20, 20–23, 25; displacement of, 15–16, 35; idealized body of, 54; Indian-ness of, erased by mascots, 79; mascots as distortions of self-images for, 81, 111, 112–113, 122, 128; mascots as pan-tribal issue for, 92; mascots as preferred over, 30; multiplicity of views on mascots, 48–49, 70, 93–102, 133n1; Noble vs. Ignoble Savage representations of, 56, 87–88; participation of, as Indian mascots, 2, 122; physical markers of, 16, 66, 73–74; pow-wows, 91; silence of, on mascot issue, 23; and white constructions Indian-ness, 55. *See also* mascots; *specific persons*
American nationalism: and male identity, 56; mythic elements of, 87

appropriation. *See* cultural appropriation
Atlanta Braves, 2
authenticity, 76, 127

Baca, Lawrence, 80
Baker, Kendall L., 57–58
Banks, Serenity J., 59
Basso, Keith H., 15
Belfielf, Clive R., 81
Bellecourt, Clyde, 109
Berkhofer, Robert Jr., 29
Black, Jason E., 75, 86
blackface, 111
Blackhawk. *See* Chicago Blackhawks
bodies. *See* physical bodies
Borchers, A. Webber, 109
Brand, Myles, 120
Brien, Bennett, 63, 64–65, 67, 122
Burns, Andy, 107, 109

Casey, Edward S., 14, 34
Chicago Blackhawks, 65–67
Chief Illiniwek: mythic origins of, 43; retirement of, as mascot, 44; Teters's criticism of, 93; Teters's protest of, 10; as topic of current study, 8. *See also* University of Illinois (UI)
Chief Noc-A-Homa, 2
Chugurupati, Sridhar, 113
civil rights. *See* protests; Red Power movement

141

About the Author

Since earning his PhD from Syracuse University, **Michael Taylor** has been researching racialized mascots and the ways in which the creators of these representations seek a connection to a desirable, idealized Indian-ness. Taylor's work on mascot imagery consists of case studies of educational institutions that are invested in such iconography. He currently holds a joint appointment in anthropology and Native American studies at Colgate University and is a member of the Seneca Nation of Indians (SNI), a tribal community located in southwestern New York State.